AF413462

# PREPARE FØR THE
# PRESSURE

# PREPARE FØR THE PRESSURE

9 STRATEGIES TO BE COURAGEOUS,
CONSISTENT, AND RESILIENT
WHEN IT MATTERS MOST

## BEN ZØBRIST

*For the One who said I was enough when the
pressure was too much to carry alone.*

# CONTENTS

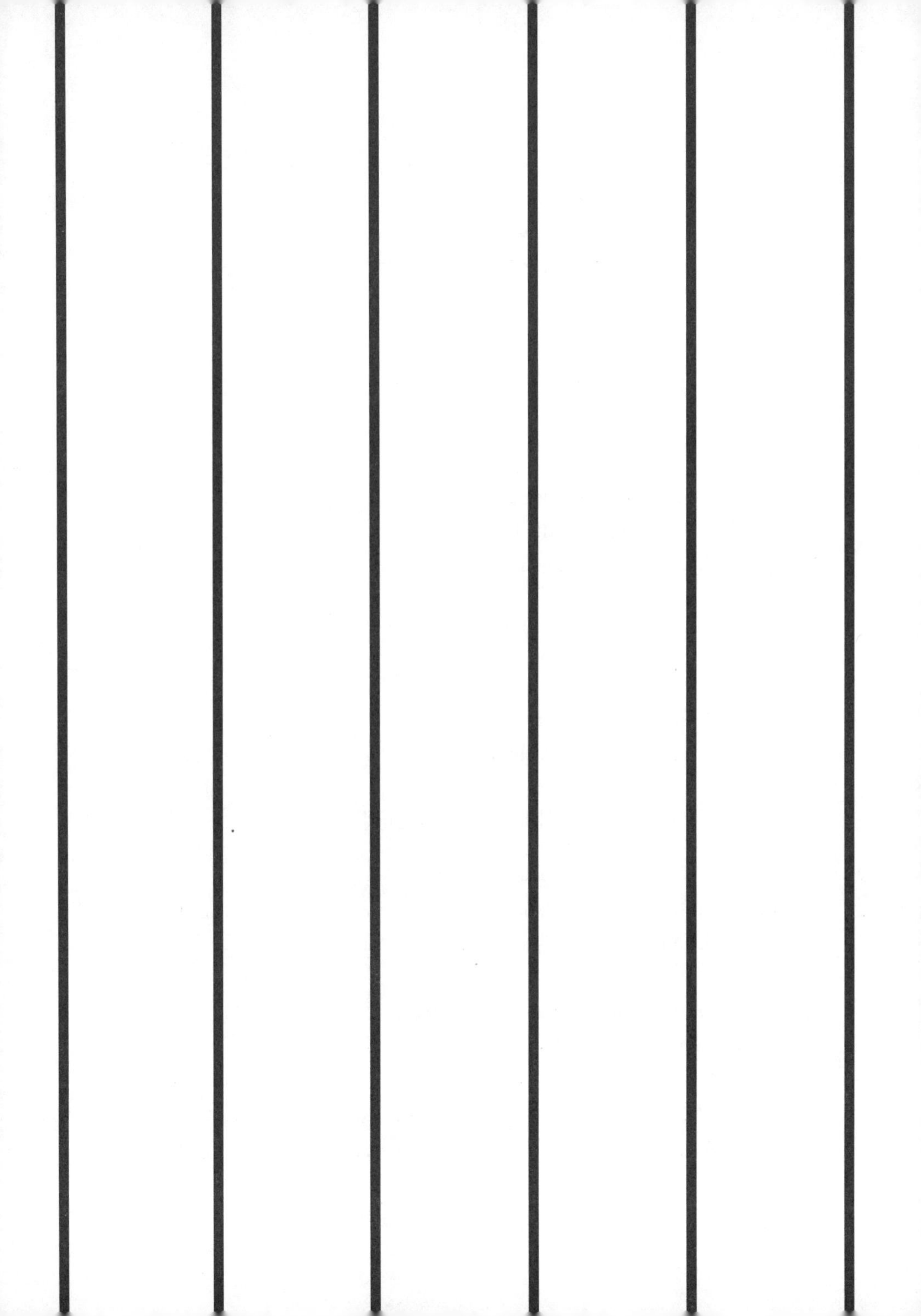

# PERFORMING UNDER PRESSURE

NOTHING COULD HAVE PREPARED ME FOR THE SINGULAR MOMENT OF my final at bat in Game 7 of the 2016 World Series between the Chicago Cubs and the Cleveland Indians. Although I'd had the incredible experience of playing in the World Series before—with Tampa Bay in 2008 and with Kansas City in 2015—playing with the Cubs in 2016 would be a moment of pressure unlike any other.

My Cubs teammates and I had clawed our way back from a three-games-to-one series deficit. After tying the series with a win in Game 6, everyone knew the final matchup would be a battle, but I had no idea that perhaps the most pressure-packed moment of my baseball career would transpire that night.

We came out of the gates hot with a fast lead in the game, but slowly the Indians fought back to tie the game late in the eighth inning against one of our best pitchers. We were so close, and now the game seemed to be slipping from our grasp. Everyone in the sports-watching world was on pins and needles as rain began to fall over the city of Cleveland, pausing the game right after the ninth inning. After a fifteen-minute rain delay, I stepped up to the plate in the tenth inning.

On one level, I knew I was ready. I'd been in tough playoff situations before. I knew how to show up in big moments. I knew what it would take to stay focused when it mattered most. And yet there was something different about this—a deep knowing that this was more than I could handle.

Physically, the details of my batting strategy were planned ahead of time through scouting and previous experience. I knew what I wanted my hands to do, when I needed to start my swing, and where I wanted the barrel to come through the zone. Mentally, I was almost unaffected in the moment—stoic, like a machine. But underneath it all was the emotion, a pit in my stomach, emerging since we'd lost the lead. The butterflies were there, but it was like I was numb to them.

I knew what it felt like to face one of the best pitchers in the World Series—I'd had that experience with Tampa Bay against Brad Lidge in our final game. Although I failed to get on base, I had still executed my plan and hit the ball hard. It was an out, but internally it had been a win.

Now, eight years later, I crouched at the plate in my stance, arms in rhythm pre-pitch, eyes fixed toward the mound, ready. I barely heard a sound despite there being tens of thousands of fans in the stands that night. I zoned in on Cleveland's pitcher, Bryan Shaw, as he released the ball.

The first pitch came at me like it had been shot out of a cannon. I knew I would take the first strike no matter what. It's a smart way to get a visual on the release point and spin of the ball. I dipped back a bit to avoid being hit by the pitch that was high and inside.

*Ball one.*

I didn't get a great look at the first pitch, so I wanted to take another just to make sure I had the timing, rhythm, and movement. I didn't swing at the next offering, which—in hindsight—was the best pitch I would see, right down the middle.

*Strike one.*

The next was a pitcher's pitch, a ball I couldn't have done anything with had I tried. It was a perfect spot for him to put it to get ahead in the count. I hoped it would be called a ball, but the ump saw it differently.

*Strike two.*

Now it was time to battle. Shaw was the kind of pitcher who knew how to throw nasty stuff, and I had to protect the plate. The fourth pitch? It was a little up and away, but with that cutter spinning back inside, I couldn't chance it. I flailed at it. Foul ball straight into the Indians' dugout. He almost snuck it by me! I remember looking up and thinking, *Make it be a strike, and put that ball on the left side of the field somewhere.*

Though the next one didn't feel like a hit with the type of swing I put on it, that just goes to show you that sometimes your approach means more than your feelings. The cutter away had my name on it. Making contact right over the outer edge of the plate, I got enough of it to push it right inside the third base-line. Cleveland's third baseman lunged for the ball, but it was out of reach. The outfielder ran as fast as he could and cut it off at the line, but not before we scored the go-ahead run and I stood on second base with a stand-up double.

Sometimes your approach means more than your feelings.

The moments when we most need to perform under pressure may or may not be on an athletic playing field. It could be in the boardroom or the classroom. In an important Zoom presentation or in a hospital surgery unit. Often the biggest moments happen in relationships—the reconnection over the phone with someone very important to you, or the moment when you finally take the risk to step toward that person who has the power to reject you. No matter the moment, there's going to be some big feelings around it.

I don't have all the answers, but I can share what has worked for me and, more importantly, what I'm still preparing for. And I'm convinced that as you develop daily rhythms of courage, consistency, and resiliency, you, too, can be prepared for the pressure.

**BATTER UP,**

# BE COURAGEOUS

IT IS OUR NATURE TO AVOID PRESSURE.

Pressure implies that something is building that we'll eventually have to deal with. Either the pressure forces us to become smaller or avoidant, or we choose to meet pressure head on. And when we try to muster our own strength to meet that pressure, there is the possibility of failure. Even if we don't fail in the moment, we may not have the energy and endurance to succeed in the long run. And with that continued possibility of failure, comes the ongoing presence of fear.

If we're honest, fear is an underlying motivation to a lot of our reactions under pressure. Many athletes get uncomfortable when we talk about fear, because in our minds it's linked to weakness. We spend a lot of energy trying to protect ourselves. Fear is a natural, primal impulse, but if we want to face pressure well, we will have to sit with this fear rather than run from it.

So what does it mean to be courageous when you feel that pressure? When you choose to be courageous, you act with clarity in the presence of fear and uncertainty. Aware of both the pressure and the fear, you still choose to meet the challenge of the moment.

Sports provide a unique crucible of sorts for us to test our courage and to see what we are made of. They provide an arena in which to grind and to grow. When we courageously show up to compete and give it our all, we still might walk home with a loss in the books. That's why it takes courage to keep coming back. But if we keep showing up, despite the loss, we will *grow*.

# 1

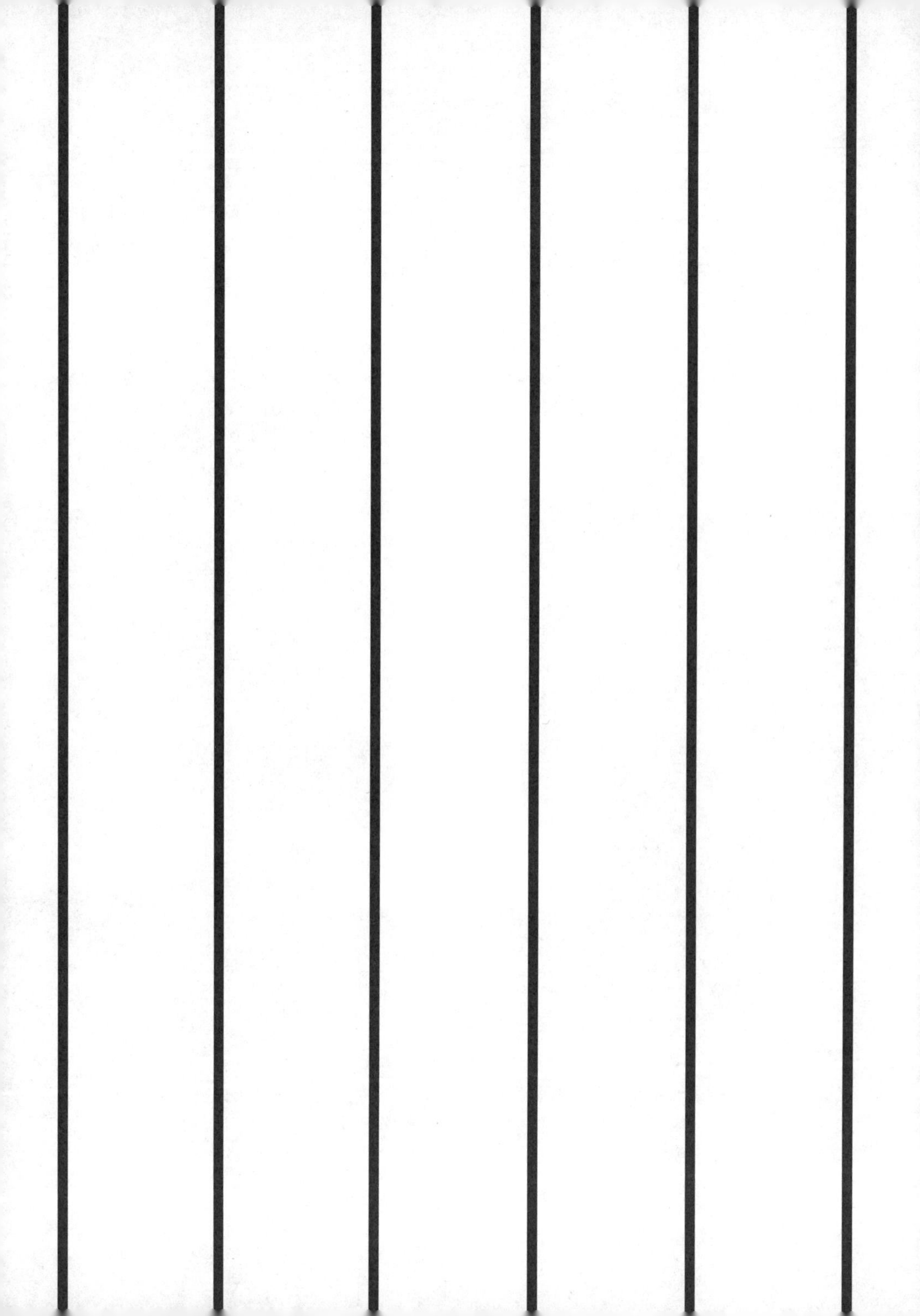

# PASSION TO PRACTICE

ROY HOBBS.

Benny "The Jet" Rodriguez.

Rudy Ruettiger.

Rocky Balboa.

My passion to compete began by watching these athletes—and those were just the heroes who had *R*s in their names! These were the characters in sports movies of the nineties who captured my imagination more than any other stories. The heartbeat of these heroes was their passion to compete for the win, their dedication and practice despite the odds, and the determination they showed in the shadows when no one was watching.

I was the little kid in Eureka, Illinois, watching Sylvester Stallone as Rocky on the screen training *hard*. What would make a guy push himself like that? Was he actually having fun? It seemed that the more I watched, the more I understood his inner toil. His opponent wasn't just Apollo; he was fighting for something bigger. He was fighting for a purpose that went beyond his passion for boxing. I'd study those scenes when the theme music hit—his muscled arms punching at the air, sweating in the silence, getting up early to chase an impossible dream no one can see.

I wanted to feel that kind of passion about something, to be willing to sacrifice when no one else would. It made sense to me that if you wanted to be able to handle the pressure under the brightest lights at night, you'd have to be willing to discipline yourself in the quiet shadows of the morning.

Rocky made me believe that what he was doing on-screen was possible in real life. I saw the passion play out in his training. The internal fire of an athlete's greatness came through the screen and into my living room. It was as if there were no cameras. No scorecard. No opposition. It was just Rocky striving. It was his will to succeed, to make something of himself—not just for himself but for everyone who supported him as well.

These movie characters—Rocky Balboa, Roy Hobbs, and Rudy Ruettiger—connected the dots for me. Could I find something I love, pursue that passion daily, and possibly become the best in the world at it? Could it happen for somebody who comes from a small town with humble means? These stories lit me up and made me believe that I could pursue a passion of my own and find more in it than I ever thought possible.

The other connection I made when I watched these stories was that *sacrifice* was necessary to be prepared to perform under pressure. I recognized that the big-time performances depended on big-time practice. Rocky had the internal drive to practice and train, and he turned that training into precision during the boxing match. I wanted the same, and I was willing to sacrifice to do it.



## The Passion to Practice

Inspired by these films, I was driven to practice with the same intensity in whatever sport I was playing at the time: baseball in the summer, basketball in the winter, football in the fall. Heck, I even got a pair of boxing gloves as a gift and accidentally punched my older sister Jess a little too hard. (We still have a picture somewhere of her black eye, which

PASSION
PREPARES
YOU FOR YOUR
PURPOSE.

eventually healed.) Then I decided to trade the boxing gloves for batting gloves and started swinging bats instead of fists. Taking swings and competing every chance I got in our small town was all I could think about. My passion to compete and the belief that I could become more led me to practice when everyone else was done.

Although I was still a little guy in junior high, my coach, Craig Gerdes, said that I had the heart of a lion. He could tell I wanted the win more than most! Truly, I hated to lose. I had an internal fire early on, the kind that moves you when nobody's watching, and it's really what shaped the competitor I became. Sports were my passion, where I felt most like myself. So it's no wonder that competition formed the earliest understanding of my identity and purpose. It wasn't *everything* to me, but it was certainly an important part of my life. And it gave me the energy I needed to push myself beyond what I was capable of at the time.

Of course, there were plenty of times when I struggled and got distracted. But my desire to experience the success I saw on the screen was my earliest motivation. I simply kept showing up regardless of how many times I failed. I learned that passion prepares you for your purpose.

What have you witnessed—whether it's an inspiring person, like Rocky, or a pursuit—that has captured your attention and given you an unusual energy? What triggers your curiosity and your desire to hear or learn more?

For some, it may be the thrill of entrepreneurship.

For others, it might be writing or painting or composing or performing.

Maybe you have a passion to find creative ways to support people who are vulnerable.

Or you might have a particular hobby that feels life-giving for you.

Identifying the interest that's uniquely yours is the first step toward finding your passion. Follow that rabbit trail. Pay attention to your curiosities, especially what you're wanting to learn more about. Whatever it is may not demand everything from you immediately, but it will begin to tug on your time and attention. Maybe it starts as an interest, and then it becomes a recreational activity you enjoy. But if it's more than that—if it's a *passion*—eventually you'll be willing to pursue it and put more effort into it.

## The Passion That Unlocks the Potential

How do you know if you've discovered the passion that's worth investing in with your time, your energy, and maybe

UNSEEN
PRACTICE
BUILDS A SENSE
OF SUCCESS
INSIDE YOU
THAT NO
TROPHY EVER
COULD.

even your money? This is what will determine whether you've identified your *real* passion or you've just found a proclivity or an interest. The answer to this question will be your guide: *Would you be willing to pursue this passion to the point of discomfort?* Would you train long enough for that passion to unlock a deeper purpose for your life? Are you willing to find your way through the shadows until your passion shows up in the light, in a meaningful way? These are the tough questions that every high achiever eventually faces when pursuing their passion.



There's an equation that has shown up again and again in my life—and in the lives of other champions I've met:

Passion + Practice + Perseverance > Pressure

*Pressure players are willing to persevere in their passion.* They have enough passion that they are willing to practice through the pain.

Your passion will likely call you into repetition; that's practice with *perseverance.* Your practice will require your energy. And this is exactly what will make you stronger than any pressure you face.

## For Those Who Are Rising

If you're a young person, or someone trying something new, I consider you to be someone who is *rising.* You're on your way. The first taste of success isn't going to be a championship trophy. It's not the plaque on the wall or the number of likes you get after a performance. The first real win you'll experience is when you discover something you love enough to practice when nobody's watching. Most of the world measures success by applause, by comparison, by outside validation. But passion isn't proven by the spotlight—it's proven in the shadows.

If you're still trying to figure out who you are and where you're going, let me encourage you: *Don't just look for the obvious wins.* Look for the moments when you feel that spark of energy, that quiet obsession that fuels your commitment to improve. *That's* the trail worth following. Passion doesn't just show up in talent; it shows up in repetition. It's not about whether you can do something once in a while—it's about whether you'll keep showing up when nobody else is asking you to.

If you practice only when it's required, you're missing the real training. But when the gym is empty, when the classroom is quiet, when the field lights are off—that's when passion proves itself. That's when you decide whether you're just *involved* in something or *invested* in it. You don't have to know if this is your "forever path" yet, but you do need to know if you're willing to own it now.

Unseen practice builds a sense of success inside you that no trophy ever could. It teaches you discipline, resilience, and confidence. And yes, it will feel lonely at times. But here's what I've learned: The moments that feel the loneliest often turn out to be the most valuable. Because that's when the dream moves from being just an idea in your head to becoming a habit in your life. Passion without practice is just hype. But passion with practice? That's *preparation*. That's what equips you to stand under pressure later.

Passion doesn't just show up in talent; it shows up in repetition.

## For Those Who Are Rooted

If you have some lived experience behind you, I think of you as someone who is *rooted*. You're firmly planted, and you have the capacity to be intentional about investing in others. If you're a coach, parent, mentor, or leader—someone who's guiding the next generation—I want to challenge your narrative. You probably already spend a lot of energy encouraging people to stay focused, disciplined, and motivated. And that's important. But what matters most is what a rising person sees in you.

People may not always listen to your words in the moment, but I promise you this—they are always watching you. They're noticing whether your spark is still alive. They see whether you've settled into maintenance mode or if you're still pursuing something that gives you energy. They pick up on whether your life is fueled by passion or just managed by obligation. Even though I'm now retired from baseball, I want my kids to see me being just as passionate about the things I am involved in today as I was when I played the game. I want them to see that passion is something that can *grow* as you get older.

Sometimes those of us who are investing in others pour so much into mentoring that we forget to *model* what it looks like to stay passionate ourselves. We exchange curiosity for responsibility. We trade our spark for busyness—even being busy investing in others! But credibility doesn't just come from giving advice; it comes from living the example. Passion is contagious—but only if it's visible.

So here's the challenge: Don't let your passion fizzle out!

While it might not look the same as it did years ago, that's okay. The next iteration may be a new version of an old love. Perhaps you'll pick up a forgotten hobby, commit to a new discipline, or create something fresh. If you're wanting to inspire passion in those you invest in, they need to see it in you. They need to see you learning, stretching, training, praying, creating—still showing up with fire in your eyes. Passion that is practiced, not just preached, becomes contagious. If you're an athlete or leader, your unseen preparation is shaping you into the kind of person who can handle pressure when it comes. If you're a parent, coach, or mentor, your lived-out passion is giving permission for the next generation to do the same.

## The Tension

Passion sounds exciting on the surface. But the real test isn't the highlight—it's the hidden work. That's where the tension lives. You feel the pull to be everywhere, say yes to everything, keep up with everyone. You want the trophy, the applause, the proof. Meanwhile, the work that actually builds you happens in silence—early mornings, empty gyms, quiet rooms, no cameras. That's uncomfortable. It can feel lonely.

It asks for sacrifice when nobody's watching and there's nothing immediate to show for it.

When passion mixes with pressure, it's easy to drift into performance mode—measuring your worth by likes, stats, or who notices. But remember, passion isn't proven by the spotlight; it's proven in the shadows. And that's the rub. Your heart wants the big moment, but your growth needs the small repetitions. You can't do it all. To say yes to what matters most, you'll have to say no to some good things. That's hard—but it's honest. And it's the doorway to real preparation.

## The Activation

Passion becomes preparation when you give it structure. Keep it simple and sustainable. Move on these three principles:

1. **Define the "one thing."** Name the pursuit that keeps tugging on your attention—the one you'd still do if nobody ever noticed. Write it down. If you're "rising," this is about focus over FOMO. If you're "rooted," this is about renewing your spark so others can see it.
2. **Design your shadow practice.** Pick a small, daily rep you can sustain (five to fifteen minutes is

enough to start). Choose a time, a place, and a trigger. (Example: "After breakfast, ten dry swings in the backyard" or "Before bed, ten minutes of writing/film study.") Protect it like an appointment.

3. **Decide your trade-offs.** Preparation requires a no. Identify one thing you'll cut this week to make space for the prep (scrolling on your phone, one hangout, an extra episode). Tell someone you trust so the boundary sticks.

Keep this equation in front of you as a mantra and a map:

Passion + Practice + Perseverance > Pressure

You're not chasing perfect; you're building endurance. Reps in the shadows create strength in the spotlight.

## The Engagement

Passion doesn't grow by accident—it grows when you give it space, when you put it into practice. Here are three ways you can lean in:

## Personal (Attention Check)

Take a few minutes and write down the one thing that keeps tugging on your attention—the thing that sparks extra energy in you. Then ask yourself: *Would I still do this if nobody ever noticed?* If the answer is yes, record one small way to start practicing it this week. It doesn't have to be huge. Just a daily rep. Just enough to prove to yourself that the fire is real—and keep it burning.

## Relational (Accountability Check)

Think about someone in your life who lives with visible passion. Maybe it's a teammate who always takes extra reps, a coach who still shows up hungry, or a friend who stays faithful in their craft. Ask them what keeps them going when nobody's clapping. Let their answer motivate you. And then model that kind of passion for somebody else. The next generation is watching more than they're listening.

## Spiritual (The Ultimate Passion)

Every morning this week, pray one simple line before you get moving: *God, give me passion that lasts longer than applause.* No long list. No pressure for outcomes. Just that. Because passion without presence will always run dry. But when you connect the fire in your heart to the Source who gave it, your practice turns into something bigger than preparation—it turns into purpose.

## Moving From Training to Trusting

Passion is a gift, but it isn't just about what lights you up in the moment—it's about where that fire comes from and who it's for. When passion is practiced in God's presence, it doesn't burn out; it gets refined. Paul wrote in Colossians 3:23–24, "Whatever you do, work at it with all your heart, as working for the Lord, not for human masters, since you know that you will receive an inheritance from the Lord as a reward. It is the Lord Christ you are serving."

That's the difference between hype and purpose. Practice in the shadows isn't wasted when you know God sees it. So don't just chase your passion for applause. Anchor it in the One who gave it to you. When you practice with Him in mind, the fire in your heart won't just fuel performance—it will carry you into purpose.

# INTENTIONAL WALK

1. What's one unseen practice you've been doing (or could start) that fuels your passion when no one's watching?

2. Where are you tempted to perform for the spotlight instead of practicing for God's presence?

3. Who around you might need to see your passion lived out consistently, not just spoken about?

2

# FAITH THROUGH THE FOG

THE LAST DAY I PLAYED WAS BITTERSWEET.

When our team got knocked out of contention after the final game, I packed my bags, tossed them in the back of my truck, and headed home. I didn't realize how much emotion I was carrying until I started driving. I didn't get far before I burst into tears—full-on, can't-catch-your-breath tears.

Surprised by my own reaction, I thought, *What's wrong with me? It's just a game.*

But the truth was, it wasn't just a game to me. I was losing a part of myself.

I'd been playing as long as I could remember, and now it was time to let it go. The transition felt like standing on a cliff with no view of what was next. God has a way of reminding us that the things we hold most dear don't really belong to us.

We're stewards: of talent, resources, relationships, and time. And eventually, our time to play runs out.

When that happens, how do we know where to go next?

The tears kept coming, sadness mixed with confusion. I had poured my heart, soul, and passion into this game. Was there purpose in any of it? I knew I had to move on, but I didn't want to. My heart still loved the game. I felt like I still had untapped potential. What I needed in that moment more than anything was faith—the faith to believe that all those years, all that energy, still had meaning. I wanted to believe that there was a grander plan at work, even if I couldn't yet see it. I had to believe there was still purpose ahead.

You might think I'm describing my last day in the majors at age thirty-eight. But the day I'm really talking about was when I was nineteen—at the end of my high school career!

At that time, I thought I was done with baseball forever. There were no scholarship offers. No open doors. I felt invisible. I believed I was capable, but I had already given the game, and my future, over to God. I told Him, "If it's over, I'll trust You with it."

And that's when *faith* became more than a word to me.

Part of my support system back then was my high school coach, Coach Gold. He believed there was more in me, even when I didn't see it. Just two weeks after graduation, he told me about a scout day. Players could pay a fifty-dollar fee, show their stuff to college and pro scouts, and at the end of the day someone might come calling. It wasn't glamorous. But though I had already let go of the dream, I figured it couldn't hurt to put on the uniform one more time. That small yes changed everything.

I could have skipped that day. I could have told myself it was wasted time and effort. But looking back, that tryout—a fifty-dollar investment—was one more step in a plan toward my future. When I didn't know where I was headed, I had friends who helped me see through the fog.

At that tryout Elliot Johnson, from Olivet Nazarene University, saw something in me too. Amid his belief, my coach's encouragement, and my parents' steady support, I began to have faith in myself. It's when I learned that sometimes faith comes through borrowed belief.

From there, doors started opening. I had the opportunities to play for all, and eventually Major League Baseball. And in a way I never could have imagined, the journey eventually led to winning a World Series and being named MVP of the Series.

It's funny, at nineteen I thought my baseball story had ended. Nineteen years later, I closed it out for real, striking out a potential Hall of Famer, Yadier Molina, in my final game with the Cubs.

Faith can take you a long way.

This said, *faith* is one of those words that gets tossed around so much it can lose its weight. But in my life, it's never been an abstract concept. Believing in a divine plan for your life is a decision to keep moving when you can't see the next step. For me, faith is clarity under pressure. It's not blind optimism or wishful thinking. It's anchored trust that's rooted in something more reliable than the scoreboard, the stat sheet, or the approval of others.

When I didn't know where I was headed, I had friends who helped me see through the fog.

## Faith and Courage Go Hand in Hand

Many people think courage means fearlessness. It doesn't. Courage is what happens when you move forward in spite of fear. And the fuel behind that courage? Faith.

Faith lets us say to ourselves:

*This moment doesn't define me.*
*I've prepared for this, even if I don't feel ready.*
*I can trust the One who sent me into it.*

Faith is fundamental to being courageous because it allows you to act with conviction, even when the outcome isn't guaranteed. It not only equips you to face a challenge but also sustains you all the way through the moment of impact.

When I was nineteen, exercising my faith didn't mean I had a guaranteed future in baseball. It meant that my heart posture shifted—from clinging to control to releasing the outcome I desired. That release gave me peace to show up for the fifty-dollar tryout without fear of failure.

## The Batter's Box: A Faith Picture

Faith is not about forcing ourselves to "feel brave." It's about aligning with a purpose bigger than ourselves so we can step forward without being owned by the result.

The flip side of faith is fear.

Fear narrows our vision. It limits us because it keeps us locked in on the worst-case scenario. Faith, though, lifts our eyes. It helps us take the next step, open the next door, embrace the next opportunity. And sometimes it lets us borrow someone else's belief until we find our own again.

I call these faith-filled friends "foggy-weather friends." (They're the opposite of fair-weather friends!) They can't see the whole path for us, but they'll walk beside us until the clouds clear. We're not meant to walk the journey alone, and these friends are gifts that help us navigate the foggiest days.

Every time we step up to perform, we exercise courage. And the reason we need courage is because we're taking a risk. *We risk failure.* We carry doubt, not knowing exactly how things will turn out.

If you've played ball, you already know that stepping into the batter's box is a lonely step of faith. It's just you, the pitcher, and the moment. If you step in with more doubt than belief, your chance of success drops. But when you step in with faith on your side—belief in your plan, in your preparation, in your God-given capability—you give yourself a real shot.

Hitting coaches often teach players to be "selectively aggressive." That means you know exactly what pitch you're looking for and you're ready to attack it when it comes. When you're being selectively aggressive, you're exercising faith to follow through, with clarity in your plan, readiness to move, and trust that your training will meet the moment.

It's the same off the field. Whatever your "batter's box" is—a tough conversation, a new opportunity, a leadership moment—stepping in with faith means you've made the choice to believe in your preparation, lean on your support system, and trust that God is working in the result, whether it's a hit or a strikeout.

## Three Anchors of Faith Under Pressure

If you want to make faith practical, especially in high-pressure environments, you need three anchors:

1.  **Faith in Yourself.** You believe you are capable of doing hard things, not because you're perfect but because you're prepared and willing.
2.  **Faith in Your Support System.** You let the right people speak belief over you when you can't find it yourself.
3.  **Faith in Your Source.** You trust God's plan more than your own performance, knowing He's writing a story bigger than your stats.

When you choose to drop these three anchors, you make your faith practical, relevant, and effective, especially in high-pressure environments.

One of the biggest misconceptions about faith is that it

WHEN WE SKIP
THE TENSION,
WE MISS THE
TRANSFORMATION.

means simply sitting back and hoping things turn out okay. But real faith is *active*. It shows up to the fifty-dollar tryout. It moves you to step into the batter's box. It makes the hard phone call. It speaks up in the meeting.

Faith doesn't mean that when I stepped into the box as a hitter, I knew I'd get a hit. It meant I believed I had the preparation, the plan, and the God-given ability to compete with confidence. And if the result was failure, it didn't shake the foundation—because faith had already won the bigger battle.

Faith doesn't replace hard work; it *strengthens* it. That's why in baseball, in business, and in life, we need the faith to follow through—to trust our preparation, our people, and our Source—and to keep swinging.

## The Tension

Faith always sounds powerful when it's part of someone else's inspiring story, doesn't it? But when it's your turn, it feels different. The inherent tension of faith is that emotional gap between wanting control and facing the unknown with open hands. It's that moment when the plan looks foggy, the results aren't guaranteed, and your heart is racing because you don't know how it's going to turn out.

That gap brings up all kinds of feelings. Fear whispers, *What if you're not good enough?* Doubt says, *You've already failed before—why would this time be any different?* Anxiety runs circles in your head, stacking worst-case scenarios until you're paralyzed. And underneath it all, there may be anger too—anger that it's as hard as it is, or that God hasn't given you a clear sign, or that other people seem to have it easier.

Most of us don't like that tension, so we cope. We distract ourselves with noise, or force ourselves into a shallow optimism, or cling to other people to give us answers they can't really provide. But all these are temporary escapes. They don't solve the tension—they just delay it.

The truth is, we must sit in the tension if we want to grow through it. Faith doesn't remove the uncertainty. It teaches us how to walk with it. When we skip the tension, we miss the transformation. And that's why the tension is worth naming—so we don't avoid it, but instead carry it with courage.

## The Activation

As I said earlier, faith isn't passive hope or blind wishing; it's an active mindset. It means retraining your mind in how you interpret the unknown. Instead of seeing uncertainty as a punishment, you start to see it as a training ground—an anchor. Anchored trust doesn't float along with your feelings. It locks in three places, which I mentioned earlier:

## 1. Faith in Yourself

Having faith in yourself means that you believe you are capable of hard things. Not because you're flawless but because you're prepared and willing to step forward. Even if the odds feel stacked against you, you remind yourself: *I've worked, I've trained, I'm ready enough to take this swing.*

## 2. Faith in Your Support System

Faith doesn't mean going alone. It means letting trusted voices remind you of who you are when you can't see it clearly. Sometimes others' belief becomes the borrowed strength that keeps you moving. Having faith in your support system means letting others speak belief into you when your own tank is empty.

## 3. Faith in Your Source

Having faith in your Source means that you trust God's plan above your own performance. Even when faith in yourself or others feels unsteady, this is the anchor that doesn't move.

When your anchor is in God, you discover that outcomes don't own you anymore. You're free to compete with courage because you trust that He is working a bigger story, whether you win or lose.

When you expand your belief beyond yourself through anchored trust, fear no longer shrinks your vision. Faith *widens* it.

## The Engagement

Now it's time to act. Faith through the fog becomes real when you put it into action. You don't just think differently—you *step* differently. Here are three ways to elevate your engagement this week:

### Personal (Heart Check)

Grab a journal or notebook and write down the one fear you've been avoiding. Name it honestly. Then, after brainstorming a few practical responses, circle one small action you can take while the fear is still there. Don't wait for the fear to disappear before you move—prove to yourself that courage isn't the absence of fear; it's forward motion in the middle of it.

### Relational (Foggy-Weather Friend)

Identify someone in your life who has believed in you when you couldn't. Reach out to them this week and thank them. Better yet, as you consider what you're facing today, let them speak into your current situation. Borrow their belief. And if you can't think of someone right now, flip it around: Decide to *be* that "foggy-weather friend" for somebody else. When you encourage another person through uncertainty, you often discover clarity for yourself too.

### Spiritual (Daily Source)

Set aside five minutes each morning this week and instead of asking God for outcomes, thank Him for His presence. No requests. No pressure for answers. Just gratitude. That posture of thankfulness shifts your heart from striving to trusting. And over time, that daily habit becomes your living well—a place where you return to get filled before high-pressure moments dry you out.

Faith through the fog isn't about guaranteeing success. It's about giving yourself the courage to step in the box again and again, no matter what happened yesterday. It's about showing up prepared, surrounded by the right voices,

Don't wait for the fear to disappear before you move.

and anchored in a Source that never runs dry. When you elevate your engagement with these small, daily steps, you build a pattern of trust that can carry you through any season of pressure.

## Moving from Training to Trusting

Have you noticed that high-pressure moments have a way of drying you out? The longer you lead, compete, or carry the weight for others, the more you feel that thirst. And in those moments, faith isn't just about believing you can— it's about believing you know where to draw from. In John's Gospel, Jesus offers this gracious invitation: "Let anyone who is thirsty come to me and drink. Whoever believes in me, as Scripture has said, rivers of living water will flow from within them" (John 7:37–38). He is showing you and me exactly where to draw from!

Faith through the fog starts with knowing the Source. Faith in yourself is important, but if it isn't grounded in faith in God, it will eventually drift into overconfidence or crumble under pressure. Faith in people around you matters too—but people are human, and naturally, their support has limits. Faith in Jesus is different. He's the only Source who can fill you without fail and keep you satisfied when every other well runs dry.

In baseball, when you're in the box, you still have to read the pitch and respond. You can't just predetermine the swing—you must discern in real time. But your preparation—your trust in your approach—is built long before that moment. Faith works the same way. You don't know exactly how every life pitch will break, but you've already decided who you trust to guide your swing.

Come to Him daily, not just in emergencies. Let His living water flow into your heart, mind, and relationships. That's how you make it to the moment *full*—and that's how you exercise faith through the fog.

# INTENTIONAL WALK

1. Where are you most tempted to rely on your own strength instead of drawing from God's living water?

2. Who in your life helps remind you to come back to the true Source when pressure is high?

3. How can you practice daily dependence on Jesus before the big "game moments" of life show up?

3

# STRETCHING FOR PERSPECTIVE

THE SUMMER AFTER MY FIRST YEAR OF COLLEGE, I JOINED UP ON A mission with Athletes in Action, a Christian organization that equips athletes and coaches to grow physically, mentally, and spiritually.[1] The mission trip was planned for Mexico and Nicaragua. Until that trip, I'd lived in relative comfort. I had never wondered where my next meal would come from or whether I'd have a roof over my head. On that trip, though, I saw kids walking barefoot on rocky roads, living in homes without doors or roofs, surrounded by trash and broken infrastructure.

But what affected me most wasn't the lack. It was the joy.

These kids had nothing—yet they had everything. They had a hunger for life. They had deep laughter. They had love. They welcomed us with open arms. They sang with everything in them, in churches made of cement and corrugated metal. I remember thinking, *They may not have what I have, but they have something I don't fully understand yet.* That trip helped me realize that performance, status, and success aren't the goal. Connection is. Purpose is. Service is. That's what really matters.

Athletes in Action used *baseball* to share love and truth and hope with people. And in that moment, I saw what sports could really be. I saw that my performance wasn't just about winning—it was a platform. A connection point. A way to bring joy and truth to others. That experience shifted the way I thought about sports.

Looking back, I realize I probably got too focused on performance at times. I wanted to win every game so badly. I wanted to be the best. But now I realize that the best part of the game was the people—the ones I played it with and the ones I got to reach because of it.

I am eager to see young people find what they're passionate about—and then find others who are passionate about it too. That's where purpose lives. Whether you are rich or poor, from America or a developing country, we all want to live meaningful lives. We all want to be brave in the face of pressure.

It might be pressure we feel to perform and excel at the work we do.

It might be the pressure we experience to care for and provide for our families.

Or maybe it's the kind of pressure we experience in athletic competition.

Whether at work, or home, or play, a lot of the pressure we feel is culture-imposed or self-imposed. God has already given us everything we need in Jesus. When we exercise faith in Him, faith in others, and faith in our own God-given abilities, we can step into courage. And that's when we're changed.



## Perspective

That pivot away from being bullied by pressure from the culture, or even from ourselves, requires a shift in perspective.

We all see the world through our own eyes, our own lens. But as we grow up, we start to realize that other people see it differently. They've lived different experiences. They feel things we don't feel. They notice things we don't notice. And if we want to grow, especially under pressure, we must learn how to see beyond our own limited view.

Years ago I watched a movie called *Vantage Point.*[2] The

whole film is this twenty-three-minute window of time shown over and over again from eight different characters' viewpoints. Same moment, totally different perspectives. It's a wild reminder: Even when something factual happens, what we see—and how we interpret it—is deeply personal.

Shifting perspective happens when we exercise the ability to zoom out to consider those other viewpoints. It doesn't mean abandoning what we see or feel, but it's being open to what someone else sees or feels too. And that takes courage—because it's uncomfortable. It stretches us. It challenges our assumptions.

I'll be the first to admit that I grew up pretty sheltered. I'm grateful for that in many ways, but I also knew that when I hit eighteen, I was going to encounter the world outside my protected bubble. And that experience outside the bubble is exactly what helped me grow—seeing things differently. Traveling. Going to college. Encountering different cultures. Having conversations with people who didn't think like me or believe what I believed. All of that required courage. But it gave me something better than comfort: It gave me depth.

And that's exactly where perspective connects to how we perform under pressure.

The pressure we feel often comes with the weight of our own perspective. We assume people are watching. We assume the moment will define us. But someone else might be in the same moment and feel none of that. That tells us: Pressure is personal. It's built on mindset. If we can learn how to shift perspective—zoom out, listen better, and ground ourselves—we become more adaptable.

The way we build that muscle is by listening to people who think differently than we do. And that ability to shift perspective *is* a muscle. One that leaders—great leaders—use often. They don't just surround themselves with people who agree. They seek out honest feedback. They ask others, "What do you see?" They know their perspective is real—but not complete.

I remember in college having hard conversations with people who didn't believe in God like I did, and I'm sure sometimes I felt attacked, because I was trying to figure out my own beliefs. But I wasn't shaken, ultimately; I was curious. I tried to be respectful of others' viewpoints, even if we disagreed. That's where faith and perspective work together. You don't have to be afraid of opposing views when your roots run deep.

So how do we gain the kind of perspective that great leaders employ?

First, start with people you trust. People who have your best interest at heart. People who've lived through seasons you haven't. One of my favorite reminders of this is my high school coach, Coach Gold. He saw something in me when I thought baseball was over. His words shifted my mindset, and that gave me options. Just staying open to his view changed my path.

You can also find perspective in wise mentors whose viewpoints may not be the same as yours, or they may not be in your court the way Coach Gold was in mine. Maybe these are older people who've made mistakes and have learned from them. Their experience is a gift. You don't have to agree with everything they say, but their stories are worth listening to. They give you more data, more depth, and more discernment.

And finally, keep your eyes open in everyday life. God will use experiences—even uncomfortable ones—to shape your point of view. Whether it's travel, sports, failure, or faith conversations, there's always something to learn if you're willing to slow down and reflect.

Here's the bottom line: If we want to live with courage under pressure, we need perspective. Whether we've been done dirty by a neighbor, or have lost a job, or have endured a life-changing injury, we need to see that we're not the center of the story. But we *are* part of something meaningful. And part of being prepared to thrive under pressure is learning how to look at life through someone else's eyes.

## The Tension

The hardest part about welcoming a fresh perspective is that it demands humility. We all want to believe our view is the whole story. To be fair, that's natural. We only know life through our own eyes. But here's the tension: When pressure hits, our limited lens often makes the moment weightier than it really is.

Pressure whispers, *Everyone is watching. This will define you. You're the center of the story.* That's why so many students crumble before a test or tryout, and why so many leaders collapse under responsibility. The weight doesn't just come from the task itself—it comes from the illusion that everything revolves around you.

Admitting that our view isn't the only one can feel threatening. For a young person, it might feel like losing identity. For a leader, it can feel like losing control. But widening your lens is not surrender. It's relief. You realize you're not alone. Others are carrying weight too. You don't have to hold the whole world together by yourself.

Expanding your perspective breaks the illusion of isolation. It reminds you that you are part of something bigger—and that relieves pressure. But you can't get there without stretching, and stretching always feels uncomfortable before it sets you free.

## The Activation

Perspective isn't an innate talent or gift; it's a skill you can practice. The mental discipline here is curious humility: choosing curiosity over assumption, even under pressure.

- **For the rising:** Curious humility might look like asking, *What am I missing?* Instead of assuming the worst, pause and listen. This doesn't mean that you are less a part of the team. It might just mean you need to learn something new in this moment so that you can become something more than you've been before.
- **For the rooted:** It's seeking honest feedback from colleagues instead of surrounding yourself with agreement. It's asking a teammate or family member, "How do you see this?" before making a decision. When you have the time to make a measured decision,

WHEN YOU
STRETCH YOUR
PERSPECTIVE,
YOU DON'T
SHRINK—
YOU GROW.

seek feedback from someone close to you. For me, it makes all the difference in the world when someone I trust shares a perspective that I have missed.

Humble curiosity doesn't weaken conviction; it strengthens it. Listening widens your perspective and builds adaptability—a skill that allows you to stay steady when pressure shifts.

The apostle Paul wrote, "I have become all things to all people" (1 Corinthians 9:22)—not because he lost himself but because he was secure enough in God to stretch toward others without breaking. For students, that means you don't have to fear being different when you walk into new spaces. For leaders, it means you can engage perspectives across generations or cultures without insecurity, because your identity is anchored.

Perspective also grows through intentional experiences. For a student, that might mean sitting with someone new at lunch or joining a volunteer trip. For leaders, it might mean traveling cross-culturally, listening to voices outside your industry, or reflecting on and considering past failures as teachers instead of enemies. Each stretch builds resilience, courage, and freedom under pressure.

# The Engagement

Expanding your perspective becomes powerful when you put it into practice. Here are ways both the rising and the rooted can stretch this week:

Personal (Expand Your Understanding)

- **For the rising:** Write down one pressure you're facing at school, in sports, or in friendships. Then ask yourself, *How might a teammate, parent, or teacher see this differently?*
- **For the rooted:** Identify a pressure point at work or home. Step back and ask, *How would my colleague, my spouse, or my child interpret this?* That shift alone can shrink the weight you feel.

Relational (Listen Before You Lead)

- **For the rising:** Have a real conversation with someone outside your usual circle—maybe a classmate who thinks differently or a sibling you often clash with. Listen without defending.
- **For the rooted:** Set aside time this week to meet with someone who challenges your perspective—a peer with different beliefs, a younger voice on your team,

or a mentor from another field. Don't argue. Ask
questions. Take notes.

Spiritual (Stretch by Serving)

- **For the rising:** Volunteer or serve in a way that places
  you outside your comfort zone—tutor a younger
  student, help someone new on your team, or serve
  alongside people who live differently than you.
- **For the rooted:** Engage in service where you're not
  in charge—join a local outreach, support someone
  quietly, or step into a space where your role is simply
  to listen and learn. Serving shifts your focus off
  performance and onto connection.

Examining your perspective under pressure loosens fear's
grip. It silences the lie that you're the center of the universe. It
opens your eyes to the bigger story God is writing all around you. I hear this in Paul's bold
announcement: "To the weak I became
weak, to win the weak. I have become all
things to all people so that by all possible
means I might save some. I do all this for
the sake of the gospel, that I may share in
its blessings" (1 Corinthians 9:22–23). Do you

see it? Paul's adaptability is a *win*, not a loss. When you stretch your perspective, you don't shrink—you grow. You become more adaptable, more courageous, and more connected. The real win isn't proving your view right. It's seeing more, loving deeper, and living freer than pressure ever allowed before.

## Moving from Training to Trusting

When Paul said he became "all things to all people," he wasn't talking about faking it or losing himself. He was talking about stretching. He was willing to step into somebody else's shoes long enough to see the world through their eyes. That takes humility. That takes courage. And that's what entertaining a fresh perspective does—it stretches you past your comfort zone so you can love people where they are.

Remember, perspective doesn't shrink you. It grows you. When you stretch toward somebody different from you, you're not losing yourself—you're finding a deeper part of who God made you to be. That's why Paul could flex his approach without losing his identity. He wasn't living for approval; he was living on mission.

And here's the good news: You don't have to wait for a crisis to practice this. You can start today—in a conversation, in your home, in your workplace, on your team. Listen before you speak. Ask questions instead of defending your point. Stretch into someone else's world long enough to see what matters to them. That's when faith gets real. That's when love takes root. That's when perspective changes everything.

# INTENTIONAL WALK

1. Where have you been stuck lately because you've been clinging to your own perspective?

2. Who is someone with a different perspective in this area that you could listen to more intentionally?

3. What's one step you can take today to notice someone else's burden and carry it with them?

SECTION 2

# BE CONSISTENT

WE'VE JUST TALKED ABOUT COURAGE—PASSION, FAITH, AND perspective—and how those three got me started on the path to living the life I was made to live. But once I stepped into college and then professional baseball, I realized those qualities had to mature. It wasn't enough just to feel inspired or supported—I needed to become *consistent*.

In professional sports, being recognized for being consistent is one of the highest compliments you can receive. The best players show up consistently—not just when the lights are brightest, but when no one's watching. That's how you earn respect. That's how you last.

I like to believe I've stayed consistent over the years,

even as my routines have changed. That's because the pressure can't be something you wait for with dread; you have to expect it with anticipation. Prepare for it. Train for it in the quiet moments, so when the time comes, you're grounded.

Consistency means you build something beneath and beyond the performance—routines, rhythms, and relationships that anchor you when the game of life gets disrupted. It's tempting to abandon the plan when you feel like you are failing or in a free fall. I've felt that way. But when I came back to my internal rhythms—the small, daily choices that were the foundation of consistency—I was able to get back on track.

Courage and consistency meet up not in perfection but in knowing how to reset. This section will give you a glimpse at how I was taught and managed to do that—although imperfectly—through focus, presence, and versatility. It's how I stayed ready when the pressure built again and again—and it's how you can too.

4

# FOCUS OVER FLASH

BY THE POSTSEASON OF 2016, I HAD BEEN SELECTED TO PLAY IN three All-Star Games and in two World Series. While these matchups might look like any other game you'd see on television, the pressure of the All-Star Game hype was completely unlike any regular season or amateur experience I'd ever had. So imagine, the tension and excitement and viewership during the World Series was like every All-Star Game on steroids! Those are the moments that players get remembered for—triumph or trial, success or failure—and it can feel like the value of your whole athletic life comes down to this culminating moment.

In Game 7 of the World Series in 2016, my focus was more locked in than ever. I knew that, after the rain delay, my part of the lineup was about to be up. In addition to all the physical preparation of scouting the opposing pitcher's video and walking through a strategy with our hitting coaches, I realized this game was going to draw from some of my emotional and spiritual resources. This wasn't just any ordinary game, and preparing for the internal battle didn't feel normal either, especially when I realized I would be coming up to bat during a key moment.

My faith was active, and I was hanging in the balance, praying to God, *Obviously, I just want to do what I'm capable of doing. I don't know what Your plan is at the end of this. I just want to stay in the moment.*

I was tuning out a lot of external noise. And I was tuning out ego on the inside—especially when they walked Anthony Rizzo, our best hitter, to get to me.

The experience taught me I could live with failure if I stuck to my process. I was beyond the part of my career where I was trying to be the hero. I knew I wasn't that guy anymore. I think every young player experiences that in big situations early in their careers. But after failing enough, you learn that there will be another shot—and the outcome isn't the point. The best competitors aren't focused on outcome, because they're locked into the process. They know what to do and how to stay focused to do it—especially when the unexpected happens.

That 2016 double meant everything to me because it validated that my process worked. The run and success with the Royals the year before hadn't been a fluke. That moment gave me the confidence not only to keep going as a player but to share this message—because maybe this process could help someone else. Not everyone realizes how long it takes to feel confident about your process—and how hard it is to stick with it when you fail.

If you want to succeed at the highest level, get comfortable building your process over time—even while you fail in some of those situations. If you can stay focused on the task at hand, and be confident in your process, you'll find yourself succeeding more often than you expected.

## Silence the Noise, Amplify the Signal

*Focus* means knowing how to respond when everything around you is noisy, uncertain, or pulling your attention in a dozen directions. One of the greatest skills I developed—through baseball, family, and faith—was learning to do what I call "silence and amplify."

First, you must *silence* the things that will distract you from your process. That might look like ignoring, avoiding, or at times directly addressing something that keeps stealing your attention. Sometimes the noise is external: pressure, performance expectations, or other people's opinions. Other times, it's internal: your ego, your fear, or your emotions trying to hijack the moment.

At the same time, you also need to *amplify* the signals that matter. What visual cues do you need to focus on? Where does your attention belong? In a baseball game, the ball is everything. So as long as my eyes, my posture, and my intent were locked in on the ball, I was in a good place.

Thankfully, this process works outside the box too!

If you have kids and one of them is talking to you and another comes in trying to interrupt, you stay focused. You not only face the first child but you look into their eyes. That's how we truly listen. That's how we give our best focus—not just a glance but our full emotional and mental presence.

When you silence distractions, you amplify the signals that matter most in the moment.

Or maybe you're going into an important interview and something is distracting you—phone notifications, or a situation at home, or even tight shoes! Silence the phone, put the home situation on pause, and, if the interview is virtual, consider kicking off those shoes. Keep eye contact with your interviewer, and focus on listening to what he or she is saying or asking you. When you silence distractions, you amplify the signals that matter most in the moment. Silence and amplify.

## Finite Focus Beats Fragmented Attention

When I was at my best, I was focused on small things. Not the stadium. Not the scoreboard. I was locked into what was most important. My feet in the box. My breath. My posture. The brim of the pitcher's cap before he delivers the ball. The seams of the baseball as it spins toward me.

The difference between focus and distraction often comes down to details. Finite focus is about being intentional with your energy—on purpose. Fragmented attention, on the other hand, feels like everything's important all at once. That's what pressure often feels like—everything swirling, every input loud.

In high-pressure moments, it's easy to lose track of the small stuff and get caught trying to feel right or look right for someone else. So we get tangled up, distracted by thinking about our appearance, or using the words we think someone else wants to hear. We must decide ahead of time what we're paying attention to—and what we're not. Without that plan, pressure will choose for us. The world will always give us more to look at. More to worry about.

And in today's world, that pressure is constant. We're so used to quick hits, swipes, and overload—social media trains us to bounce from one thing to the next. We lose our ability to sit in the moment. Overcoaching, overstimulation, and too many voices can paralyze even the most talented players. That's why simplifying our focus—and clarifying what we're ignoring—is so important.

## Build Spiritual and Mental Trust

When I remember the way that I built focus, I recall my childhood. I was raised in a big, loud family with lots of opinions. And we were always around people—at church, in the community, and at ballparks. I had to learn early on how to get things done in a noisy environment. Whether it was memorizing verses at Sunday school while ten other kids were chattering around me, or locking in on a play while a coach was yelling, I had to train myself to focus on one voice, one cue, one task.

And that didn't happen just because I was disciplined. It happened because I trusted something deeper. Focus isn't just about discipline; it's about surrender. If you're trying to focus in your own strength all the time, you'll wear out. Eventually, you have to let go of your need to be perfect and trust the process, even when you fail.

Spiritual focus, for me, has always helped with this because it turns my attention to the Source. I'm not the one who determines how much pressure I'll face or whether I'll succeed in the moment. That's God's job. My job is to be faithful with the process. To trust that my preparation has purpose—regardless of the outcome.

That kind of trust takes years to develop. But the players, parents, and leaders I've seen succeed long term are the ones who learn to trust without needing full control. They know what they're focused on. They believe in their process. And they're not shaken when things don't go according to plan.

## The Tension

Unfortunately, in these critical high-pressure moments, there's likely more noise than there are important cues and signals that we want to focus on. Pressure multiplies

REAL
FOCUS IS
SUBTRACTION,
NOT ADDITION.

distractions and fears until you feel like you're drowning in it all. The scoreboard. The critics. The what-ifs. The phone notifications. The endless comparisons. Inside your head, doubts whisper, *You're not enough. You're falling behind. Everyone else has it together but you.*

That's what pressure does: It makes the swirl louder. For those who are rising, it might be the anxiety of schoolwork, social media, or a big performance. For those who are rooted, it might be the flood of emails, deadlines, family expectations, and the responsibility of guiding others.

Here's what I want you to remember: Focus has to be limited. When you try to focus on everything, you focus on nothing. Fragmented attention drains your energy, makes you reactive, and keeps you stuck in the swirl. The challenge is to give yourself permission to not give attention to everything. But that feels risky, because ignoring something feels like dropping the ball. Real focus is subtraction, not addition. It's choosing what to silence so you can strengthen what matters most.

## The Activation

Focusing effectively isn't about gritting your teeth harder. It's about being intentional about finite focus—deciding in advance what will receive your attention and what won't.

- **For the rising:** Imagine you're studying for a big test or stepping onto a field. The swirl of distractions—texts, Instagram, crowd noise, your own nerves—all scream for attention. Finite focus means you decide ahead of time, *In this moment, I'm focused only on the question in front of me . . . on the ball in front of me . . . on the next step in front of me.* I would focus on the seams of the baseball and how they were spinning even as the ball was being thrown around the infield while I was on defense. When you get that locked in, everything else gets quiet.
- **For the rooted:** At work, at home, or while mentoring others, distractions multiply too. The inbox, the metrics, the critics, the comparisons. Finite focus means telling yourself, *Right now, I'm focused only on this conversation with my child . . . this project . . . this person sitting across from me.*

Often work and social media on my phone become a distraction from what I need to be focused on at home. If one of my kids wants my attention and I'm locked in to my phone, I must actively put down the phone, turn my eyes and shoulders toward them, and look into their eyes to focus on what they're saying. It's not an easy transition, but it's the right one. I'm not perfect at it, but I know it's important and is a skill I need to consistently practice.

Finite focus simplifies the swirl. It replaces fragmented attention with clarity.

You realize you can't control the whole storm, but you can choose where to set your eyes. And where your eyes go, your life follows.

## The Engagement



Focus becomes powerful when you practice it consistently. Here are three parallel ways for those who are rising and those who are rooted to live it out:

Personal (Silence the Distraction)

- **For the rising:** Turn off one notification on your phone for a set period—maybe Snapchat, TikTok, or gaming alerts. Use that space to focus on one meaningful task or even a moment of quiet.
- **For the rooted:** Model this discipline. Close your inbox, mute Slack, or put away your phone for an hour. Replace distraction with something intentional:

Scripture reading, journaling, or finishing one task with focus.

## Relational (Keep Your Eyes Up)

- **For the rising:** In one conversation this week, put your phone down and give a friend, teammate, or parent your full attention. Look them in the eyes. Listen without rushing to respond.
- **For the rooted:** In your next meeting, practice, or family interaction, silence all devices and offer your full attention. Eye contact and presence communicate, *You matter. I'm here.*

## Spiritual (Reset Your Focus)

- **For the rising:** Each morning, write down one lie you've believed—thoughts such as *I'll never measure up*—and then write one truth from Scripture or encouragement that counters it. Carry it with you through the day.
- **For the rooted:** Begin your day by naming what you need to silence. For instance, *It's all on me*—and amplify what God has spoken: "My grace is sufficient for you" (2 Corinthians 12:9). Pray that truth over yourself and over those you're guiding.

Having focus under pressure doesn't happen by accident. It's built through small, repeated choices. Silence the noise. Fix your eyes. Anchor in truth. And when the lights are brightest—whether it's a championship game, a final exam, a boardroom presentation, or a family crisis—both those who are rising and those who are rooted will stand steady. Not because the swirl disappeared, but because you've trained your focus on what matters most.

## Moving from Training to Trusting

When you're under pressure, it's easy to fix your eyes on the problem. The opposition. The fear. The noise. But a word from the book of Hebrews describes a shift we can make. The author wrote, "[Let us fix] our eyes on Jesus, the pioneer and perfecter of faith. For the joy set before him he endured the cross, scorning its shame, and sat down at the right hand of the throne of God" (12:2). Jesus didn't focus on the shame or the suffering. He focused on the joy that was coming. He saw the full picture—and stayed locked in on the mission.

That's the challenge for us too. When pressure rises, what do we fix our eyes on? What pulls our attention? What fills our headspace?

Effective focus is learning to silence certain things and amplify others. Silence the lies. Silence the shame. Silence the voice that says you're not enough or it's all on you. Then amplify truth. Amplify grace. Amplify who Jesus is and what He's already done for you.

His posture was one of humble obedience and courageous endurance—and that's the same posture we're invited to take. Not because we're strong enough but because He already went before us.

Having focus under pressure doesn't happen by accident.

# INTENTIONAL WALK

1. What's pulling your focus right now that you need to silence?

2. What's one truth you need to amplify this week?

3. How does Jesus' example help you keep your posture steady under pressure?

5

# PRESENCE OVER PERFECTION

"NEVER LET THE PRESSURE EXCEED THE PLEASURE."

These words were spoken to me by legendary major-league manager Joe Maddon, who managed me for all but one of my major league career years. If there's one thing he consistently brought to the table—whether we were winning, losing, under the radar, or under the lights—it was this: the ability to stay present.

Joe's words to me about pressure were his reminder to keep the game fun. Even though we were professionals, getting paid a lot of money to do a difficult job in front of the world, he never wanted us to forget how to keep it light. He knew that tension kills timing. He wanted the joy to outweigh the weight.

Joe also had a unique perspective on the nature of

pressure itself. He didn't see it as a threat. He saw it as an indicator—a sign that you were right where you were supposed to be. Expectations were actually a good thing, not something to run from. Pressure is proof you have something meaningful in front of you.

I remember a specific moment early in my big-league career when Joe's presence and belief helped settle me during a storm I wasn't ready for. It was back in 2006, when I was playing for the Tampa Bay Rays. I had just been called up and started my first few games going 0 for 13 at the plate. Eventually, I got my first hit—a blooper off Curt Schilling—but even after that, I still wasn't finding my footing. I was hitting around .200 or below—uncharted territory for me. I'd always been a .300 hitter. It had never taken me that long to get comfortable. But this was different. The level of opposition was higher. The margin for error was thinner. And the pressure—both external and internal—was unlike anything I'd faced before.

We were on a road trip out west, and I remember feeling the weight of it one day before the game. Joe could see it in me, in my body language—the way I was moving, carrying myself, even during early work. I was overworking, trying to grind my way into confidence.

Joe didn't ignore it. He walked out to shortstop while I was taking ground balls and gave me what I call *borrowed belief.* Just like Coach Gold did for me years earlier, Joe spoke something over me I wasn't sure I believed yet.

"Ben," he offered, "I've seen a lot of major-league players over a lot of years. You just have to believe me on this: You're going to play in this league for ten years. Trust me. I know good players—and you're one of them."

I'll be honest—I thought he was a little crazy when he said that. I was just trying to survive the week, trying to figure out how to stay up. Ten years? I couldn't even see the next Tuesday.

But he saw something in me. And more important, he made time to speak it. He could've been back in the office doing his own prep for the game that night. But instead, he walked onto the field and found a struggling rookie—not to critique or correct, but to give me a moment of peace, a spark of optimism, and some hope that would carry me through the weight I was feeling.

That moment didn't suddenly fix my swing. I still struggled for the better part of those two months. And honestly, there were tough stretches in 2007 too. But that moment planted something in me—a seed of trust, a recognition that this manager wasn't just going to *grade* me. He was going to fight for me. And that made all the difference.

Later in my career, Joe did it again—this time with another player. We were still with the Rays, and it was the final game of the 2011 season. Dan Johnson was on our roster, and he was a guy who'd had a great year in the minors but hadn't had a hit in the big leagues since coming back up in September. Not one ball had landed for a hit in weeks. But with two outs in the bottom of the ninth—and the entire season on the line—Joe pinch-hit Dan Johnson. And he delivered!

That swing tied the game and led to one of the most unforgettable comeback wins in baseball history. But to me, it was more than a bold call. It was Joe being Joe—staying present, reading the moment, trusting his gut, and choosing belief when stats said otherwise.

That's the kind of leader I try to be now. Someone who's not adding more pressure but who is helping younger players carry what they're already feeling. Someone who says the thing that balances the weight instead of adding more to it.

Ten years after that first road trip, I was still playing. And I was still playing for Joe. In that memorable Game 7 of the 2016 World Series—when pressure had every reason to win—I stepped up to the plate already grounded. Because years earlier, Joe had shown me that pressure can be transformed by staying present.

When you're in the middle of a high-pressure moment, it feels like you have to be perfect. But the truth is, that pressure to be perfect pulls you away from the present—and presence is the skill of learning to return to your training. Presence is about being aware. It's about noticing when your attention drifts and learning how to bring it back. Your body is in the moment, but your thoughts might be in the past, the future, or somewhere else entirely. Presence is the awareness of those misalignments—and the commitment to come back into unity. Presence is when your body, your mind, and your spirit are in the same room at the same time.

Presence isn't just about locking in at the jump; it's about returning to what matters after we stumble. Over time, I learned to align my focus not just physically but emotionally and spiritually too. Great leaders and high performers embrace this process all the time. They know how to come back to their breath, their values, their game plan. That's where consistency is born—not in perfect execution but in perfect return.

Being consistent doesn't mean going 4 for 4 every day. It means noticing when you're off and finding your way back to center. It means understanding when your timing, attitude, or mechanics are drifting—and having the habits to correct yourself midstream.

Focus helps you notice the drift. But those habits that help you return to center—like breathwork, anchors, phrases, posture resets—are the meat and potatoes of presence.

Sometimes people see me sitting still and think I'm calm. But often, my mind is racing. I'm mentally creating or processing, so I need my body to be still. That's one form of alignment. In other moments, though, the pressure calls me to activate all three: my body, mind, and soul.

And that's when presence becomes trickier.

Because there are three ways our attention can run away from the present:

- Into the past: replaying mistakes or feeling shame
- Into the future: obsessing over outcomes, fear, or expectations
- Into the noise: external distractions, critics, or our phone

Presence requires more than willpower. It's more than a mental exercise. It requires practice. It requires us to live it out *in our bodies.* We've got to feel the ground beneath our feet. Feel the breath in our lungs. Get back into our bodies. Reclaim now.

This way in which we can be removed from the present moment is one of the biggest challenges facing the younger generation—and facing me too. Don't let someone else's highlight reel steal your moment. Don't let distraction rob your depth. Learn to reenter your own story, in your own space, with your own breath.

Mindfulness matters. Because when you're so practiced in presence that it becomes regular—when you can return repeatedly to your process, your values, your purpose—you begin to feel hope. And not just false hope, like the kind that lives in the clouds and disappears when life gets hard. I'm talking about grounded hope. Hope rooted in trained awareness. In spiritual truth. In practical, repeatable renewal. That's the kind of hope that carries you through pressure. And that's why presence isn't just a nice idea. It's not a soft skill. It's a survival skill for when your mind feels disconnected from your body. When your spirit feels distant from your decisions, presence is the pathway back. You can handle pressure—not by escaping it but by returning to what grounds you.

## The Tension

When I think about my biggest failures, I still remember what it felt like to be absolutely *gutted* in those moments. Pressure doesn't just scatter our attention—we can feel it all over our bodies. It feels like we're missing our own lives while it's happening. Because if we're stuck in the past, we're not experiencing the present.

For the rising, that tension can show up as shame over a mistake in a previous game, dread of an exam or audition, or the fear of not being enough in friendships or school. For the rooted, it often presents as the weight of leadership—balancing responsibilities, caring for family, or mentoring others while feeling stretched too thin.

The emotions are real:

- Frustration: *Why can't I just stay locked in?*
- Shame: *I must be weak for getting distracted.*
- Restlessness: that constant hum that never lets you feel settled.

- Sadness: the sense that you're physically present but emotionally absent.

What's needed in those moments isn't more toughness or perfection. What's needed is permission to return. Permission to breathe, to reset, to release the pressure of always being "on," and to step back into the moment with hope. Presence requires gentleness toward yourself—the grace to say, *I drifted, but I can come back.*

## The Activation

Presence isn't about never drifting; it's about learning to return quickly. The skill here is returning to awareness—the ability to notice when your body, mind, and spirit are out of alignment, and to bring them back together. Here are some things to pay attention to:

**Body:** Notice your breath, posture, and physical cues. Pressure tightens your body; presence loosens it.

**Mind:** Notice when your thoughts race backward into regret, forward into fear, or outward into noise. Then call them back.

**Spirit:** Notice when your heart feels disconnected from God or your values. Presence means inviting your soul to reenter the moment with faith and hope.

- **For the rising:** This awareness might mean catching yourself zoning out during a practice or conversation and choosing a quick reset instead of spiraling into shame.
- **For the rooted:** It may mean recognizing distraction in a meeting or at home and modeling a calm reset for those you lead.

For instance, I often have to catch myself while driving in Nashville when I notice I'm frustrated with traffic or things going on around me. For me, that presence begins with feeling the emotion of frustration and admitting that it's getting to me. If I start there, it's usually easier to pause and see what I could do to bring calm to the chaos.

This is why hope and optimism are so tied to presence. Hope gives us courage to return instead of running away. Optimism opens our eyes to possibility instead of pressure. Over time, awareness becomes a habit that steadies us during slumps, storms, or high-stakes moments.

Jesus doesn't shame us for drifting—He invites us to return: "Come to me, all you who are weary and burdened, and I will give you rest" (Matthew 11:28). Presence isn't grinding harder but trusting deeper. It's finding rest—not in perfect control but in the One who carries the weight with you.

## The Engagement

Presence becomes real when you put it into practice. Here are three ways both the rising and the rooted can engage this week:

Personal (Return to Now)

- **For the rising:** When you catch yourself drifting into the past or future, practice a one-breath reset. Inhale slowly, exhale fully, and say to yourself, *Right here, right now.* Repeat three times.
- **For the rooted:** Model this reset in your own high-pressure moments—pausing in the car before a meeting or resetting between family conversations. Let those you lead see that drifting isn't failure; returning is strength.

WHEN
PRESSURE
MEETS HOPE,
PRESSURE
LOSES.

Relational (Be Present with People)

- **For the rising:** In your next important conversation—with a teammate, parent, or friend—put away your phone and give your full attention. Look others in the eyes, notice their tone, and listen all the way through.
- **For the rooted:** Start by modeling keeping your phone off and put away in the presence of those you lead, showing them that your attention is fully on them and not on all the other responsibilities you have.

Spiritual (Return to Rest)

- **For the rising:** Each evening, reflect on one moment when you drifted and one moment when you returned. Thank God for both—the drift shows your need; the return shows His nearness.
- **For the rooted:** End your day by expressing gratitude to God over where He helped you return. Then pray the same covering for those you influence. Presence multiplies when it's both practiced and passed down.

Presence isn't a luxury. It's survival under pressure. It doesn't mean you never drift—it means you always come back. The more you practice returning, the faster you recover, and the stronger your hope becomes.

Over time, you'll discover what Joe Maddon modeled: Pressure doesn't have to rob you of your joy. And when pressure meets hope, pressure loses.

## Moving from Training to Trusting

Choosing presence over perfection is saying yes to the invitation Jesus offers:

> Come to me, all you who are weary and burdened, and I will give you rest. Take my yoke upon you and learn from me, for I am gentle and humble in heart, and you will find rest for your souls. (Matthew 11:28–29)

Staying present is a way to release the burdens that distract and to practice trust.

Jesus doesn't just tell us to perform

under pressure—He invites us to return to Him when the pressure gets heavy. He doesn't shame us for being tired. He doesn't judge us for being distracted or distant. He simply says, *Come back. Learn from Me. Rest with Me.* And that's what presence is: It's a return. A return to who He is . . . and a return to who we are in Him.

When the weight gets real—whether it's performance expectations, personal fears, or emotional fatigue—our instinct is often to push harder or hide deeper. But Jesus offers another way. His yoke isn't light because life is easy. It's light because He carries it with us.

In a world that tells us to be more, do more, and post more, this is the invitation that changes everything: *Come back. Learn from Me. Let Me walk with you.*

When you start practicing presence with Jesus, it doesn't mean the pressure disappears. It means your soul doesn't have to carry it alone. And in that space—where your spirit rests and your shoulders drop—you'll find something better than hype. You'll find *hope.*

# INTENTIONAL WALK

1. What weight have you been carrying alone that Jesus is inviting you to share?

2. When pressure hits, what do you usually turn to first—and does it help you stay grounded?

3. Practically, how could you invite Jesus into the next pressure-filled moment instead of pushing Him to the side?

6

# VERSATILITY OVER VOLUME

AS A YOUNG UP-AND-COMING BIG LEAGUER IN 2008, I KNEW HOW TO be a shortstop, which was my primary position at the time—that's how I was seen—but I wasn't yet confident that I was a *major-league* shortstop. Not because of my defense but because of my hitting. My numbers in my first year and a half in the big leagues weren't enough to hold that starting job. I'd been a strong hitter at the minor-league level, but the jump to the majors is the biggest there is, and I was still learning.

So during that offseason, I worked my tail off on my swing. I focused on finding a way to hit at the major-league level—I was not thinking about playing other positions. I had some new cues in my swing that I believed could unlock more power, and I was looking for a way to showcase it.

That's when Joe Maddon called before spring training.

We had just traded for Jason Bartlett from the Minnesota Twins—a proven big-league shortstop, offensively productive and defensively dependable. Joe told me they were hoping I'd take on a utility role, playing a variety of defensive positions.

My first response was curiosity: *Will this mean fewer opportunities, or is this a way to make my mark?* I believed in Joe—he had already told me he saw me playing ten years in the big leagues—so I trusted that this could be a path to making an impact.

And truthfully, I was ready for a change. The Rays had been a doormat in the AL East, getting pounded by the Yankees and Red Sox. If putting Jason Bartlett at shortstop and me in a utility role gave us a better chance to win, I was in.

That spring, I went all in. I carried every glove I owned. I ran from shortstop to second to third, even first. I jumped into the outfield for fly balls whenever there was an opening. Wherever the starting guys weren't taking reps, I slid in behind them to get work. I wasn't always confident early on—I wanted to make sure I could be a major-league defender everywhere—but I was in a rush to gain experience.

Unfortunately, I broke my thumb when I landed hard while running the bases a few weeks into camp. I couldn't catch a ball, but I could still run around during batting practice and keep learning these spots. It's always disappointing to lose the chance to earn a spot on the team, but I was determined to get back quickly. When I returned, I got sent to Triple-A—and they put me everywhere. That utility experience became my ticket back. My bat was showing more power, my defense was versatile, and by the end of 2008, I was getting opportunities on a team that went from worst to first and all the way to the World Series.

That season taught me something huge: Being a utility player didn't mean being less important. It meant being a different kind of important.

Over time, that role grew into what people called "super utility"—a starter who bounced between positions to give the manager maximum flexibility. By the time I joined the Cubs in 2016, I was known for it. It's what allowed Joe Maddon—once again—to slide me from starting second baseman during the All-Star Game to playing left field in Game 7 of the World Series so Javy Báez could start at second.

What people sometimes forget is that versatility doesn't happen by accident. It's a choice—one that starts with healthy humility. Back in 2008, I could've dug in my heels,

VERSATILITY
IS A WINNING
MINDSET.

insisted that I was a shortstop, and fought the move. But Jason Bartlett was better at that position at the major-league level, and I accepted that. Again, not as a diminished role but as a different role.

When you can shift your mindset and your position for the sake of the team, you make everyone around you better. And when the team gets better consistently, you do too. Versatility is a winning mindset. It helps you win. And it helps everyone else win with you.

## Consistency Is Being the Same Person— Not Being in the Same Spot

Versatility isn't just about moving around to different spots or wearing multiple hats. It's the ability to adapt without losing who you really are. You're not doing everything—you're doing what's needed and doing it well enough that it lifts the overall performance and takes pressure off the team. At school, a group project, you may offer your organizational strengths, tech expertise, or design skills to make the outcome a win for the group. In the office, you might support a coworker by using your unique skill set in a way that benefits the whole team. At home you might jump in on a chore, yard work, cooking, or car maintenance for the good of the family.

True versatility starts with having a heart for the team and what it's trying to accomplish. It's rooted in healthy humility, the kind that says, *I might not be the best person for this particular job, but I'm capable, and if shifting to this position makes us better, I'm willing.*

Toxic self-pity says, *I'm not good enough anywhere.* Healthy humility says, *I may be limited in some ways, but I'm still very valuable to the team.* If you can carry that mindset, your value will grow as you grow—because you're willing to shift to different roles without losing yourself.

Being ready to help where you're needed most takes an open mind. Experience matters, but so do readiness and steadiness. You might think that versatility could make you *less* consistent—changing roles means losing rhythm. But consistency isn't about the role you're in; it's about the person you are.

Can you bring the same energy, the same openness to growth, and the same mindset no matter the role or challenge? In high-pressure environments, things are always changing. The opposition changes. The plan changes. The personnel changes. But if you've trained your mind to be versatile, you can handle those changes without losing your edge—and sometimes even thrive in them.

That's how I adapted to different roles throughout my professional career. I chose to see those shifts not as obstacles but as opportunities—to make myself more valuable to the team and more prepared for the big moments. Coaches and leaders trust those who are ready to take on whatever challenge is at hand, because they know those people won't disrupt the plan or complain about the change. They'll just be ready.

A versatile person carries humble confidence into every shift. Though you may not have all the experience in a new role, you believe you're capable of contributing. And at the end of the day, even if you didn't come through in every way, you came through in some way. That means walking into the clubhouse prepared for change—knowing the lineup could shift before the first pitch. And if you're ready for things to change at 2:00 p.m., you'll handle the changes at 8:00 p.m. in front of forty thousand people a lot more smoothly. Teammates respect that. People respect that. Because everybody knows it takes every single person pulling their part of the rope to come through in the clutch.

In the 2016 postseason, I rarely played second base—even though I'd started at second in the All-Star Game just months earlier. That didn't bother me. The beauty of versatility is that your identity isn't tied to one role. It's tied to your mindset, to how you answer the call when the role shifts. That kind of mindset builds confidence even in the middle of constant change.

Some people confuse versatility with doing more. But that's *volume*, and volume burns you out. Versatility isn't about proving you can do everything; it's about doing the right thing right now. It's not an adjustment to impress; it's an adjustment to serve.

If you're taking on new roles just to prove something to yourself or others, you'll eventually make it about you. But if you take on new roles to make the team better, that changes everything. For me, it's about being the best version of myself wherever I'm placed—the best version of me in left field, at second base, in the clubhouse, or interacting with fans. The best version at home, and in my church, and in my neighborhood. It's not about doing more; it's about shifting faster, with less resistance.

If I were talking to a young athlete or a new business leader, I'd tell them that so much of our twenties and thirties is about being willing to adjust. In the business world or any high-pressure environment, we must adapt faster than others. We need to be willing to do the things other people don't want to do.

When you take on that mindset, the people making the decisions start to see you as dependable. Not because you're perfect. Not because you're great at everything. But because you're willing, you're ready, and you're prepared. You're building a work ethic, a steady identity, and a consistent effort. Success is not about being consistently great—it's about being consistently grateful for the opportunity and doing your best to make the most of it.

## The Tension

The emotional tension of versatility is that it can feel like losing yourself. When you're asked to shift roles—to step out of the spotlight, hand off a title, or take on a role that feels smaller or less glamorous—the first emotions that rise are fear and insecurity: *Am I less valuable now? Will people forget me? Does this mean I've failed?*

For the rising, this often feels like frustration when a

coach benches you or when you're asked to play a different position than the one you trained for. It might be stepping into a new role or giving up a spotlight to let someone else shine. And for the rooted, the tension may show up as being asked to adjust at work, take on behind-the-scenes responsibilities at home, or mentor someone else into a role you once held.

> The stretch hurts before it heals.

There can be pride, comparison, and jealousy in those shifts. Emotionally, versatility can feel like surrendering something you earned. But versatility doesn't shrink you—it stretches you. And the stretch hurts before it heals. The challenge is learning to accept a different role without interpreting it as a lesser role. What's needed is courage—the courage to walk with humility, trusting that your value isn't shrinking. It's simply being redirected.

## The Activation

Again, versatility isn't about doing everything or being everything to everyone. It's about showing up as the same steady person no matter what role you're asked to play. It is anchored identity—shifting your identity from *position* to *person*.

- **For the rising:** Consistency doesn't mean you always get the position you want. It means teammates, teachers, or friends know they can count on you to bring effort and the right attitude, with humility, wherever you're placed. Being benched or moved doesn't erase your value—it reveals your ability to stay steady under pressure. I can't tell you how many times I showed up for a game, only to play a different position than I thought I'd be playing. It wasn't comfortable, but I tried to show up with the same effort and preparation.
- **For the rooted:** For parents, coaches, and leaders, consistency means having the same character whether you're leading in the spotlight or serving behind the scenes. People trust you not because you do everything perfectly but because you're steady, adaptable, and willing. Being dependable goes a long way in building loyalty and trust if you are a coach or a parent. I may not always be the most dependable, but it's what I aim for wherever I am, rather than insisting on the position that everyone looks at.

This is the mindset of healthy humility. Toxic shame tempts with, *I'm not good enough anywhere.* Pride shouts, *If it's not the best role, I want no part of it!* But healthy humility says, *I'm valuable wherever I'm placed, because my worth isn't tied to the position; it's anchored in who I am.*

The role that feels small may be the one God uses most. The unseen work, the sacrifice, the shift that helps someone else shine—all of it matters. Pressure will tempt you to cling to status, but humility opens your eyes to the bigger mission. That's why versatility is such a strength under pressure: It makes you flexible without losing your identity, adaptable without insecurity, and humble without being weak.

## The Engagement

Versatility takes root when you act on it. Here's how you can practice this week:

Personal (Stretch the Role)

- **For the rising:** Think of one place where you've clung tightly to "your spot"—maybe a sports position, a classroom role, or a social group. Choose one way to adapt for the sake of others: Step into a supporting role, learn a new skill, or back up someone else.

- **For the rooted:** Notice where you've been protective of your tasks or influence—at work, in family roles, or in mentoring. Practice flexing by delegating, covering for someone, or allowing someone else to lead while you support.

## Relational (Serve the Team)

- **For the rising:** This week, intentionally take a role that allows a teammate or peer to shine. Cheer for someone else's win. Do the task no one else wants. Discover the paradox that when you give up the spotlight, your influence often grows.
- **For the rooted:** Create space for other voices. Encourage a student, child, or teammate to step forward while you step back. Let them try their way without micromanaging. Model what it looks like to lead by serving.

## Spiritual (Shift with Faith)

- **For the rising:** Begin your day with a prayer of flexibility: *God, wherever I'm placed today, help me serve with humility and joy.* Reflect in the evening: *Did I resist with pride or embrace with faith?*

- **For the rooted:** Pray for flexibility, but also pray it over those you influence. Thank God for unseen opportunities to serve. Ask Him to anchor your worth in faithfulness, not visibility.

> Versatility doesn't erase your value—it multiplies it.

Versatility doesn't erase your value—it multiplies it. The more willing you are to shift roles, the more valuable you become to the team and the more you discover who you are apart from titles.

Under pressure, versatility is humility in action. It announces, *It's not about my position—it's about our mission.* And often, the role you didn't want becomes the role that prepares you for your greatest impact later.

## Moving from Training to Trusting

In God's kingdom, value is never measured by position or title. The roles that seem less visible often carry the greatest weight. That's what Paul was saying in his letter to the believers in Corinth: "The body is not made up of one part but of many. . . . Those parts . . . that seem to be weaker are indispensable" (1 Corinthians 12:14, 22). It's easy to think the most important role is the one in the spotlight. But God designed the body—and teams—so that every part matters. Sometimes the most valuable thing you can do is shift quietly into a role that allows someone else to thrive. That's not losing value. That's multiplying it.

In baseball, that might look like moving from your favorite position so the team can win. In life, it might look like serving behind the scenes so someone else can step into their calling. Either way, the scoreboard doesn't tell the whole story—the health of the body does.

God doesn't reward volume. He blesses faithfulness. The question isn't, *How many roles can I play?* It's, *Am I ready to play my role today, whatever that role may be?*

When you embrace healthy humility and a heart for the team, you're not just preparing for a moment—you're preparing for the life God has called you to live.

# INTENTIONAL WALK

1. Where are you clinging to a role or title instead of embracing the opportunity to contribute in a new way?

2. Who around you could be lifted up if you shifted to a new role?

3. How can you prepare your heart this week to serve wherever God places you?

# BE RESILIENT

EVEN THOUGH WE'VE SPENT TIME LEARNING HOW TO STEP INTO THE challenge of pressure with courage and how to build consistency in riding its current, the questions remain: Is this sustainable? How long can we bear the weight of preparation, performance, and pressure?

This is where *resilience* comes into play.

Resilience is more than gritting our teeth and bearing it when the pressure keeps coming. It's more than the weight we carry from past lessons learned or grit we've gained. Often, we carry weight we don't even realize—situations we've avoided, old wounds, quiet fears, unspoken expectations. If we don't deal with these things, pressure will make them louder, making it harder to stay courageous and consistent over the long haul.

Ultimately, we want to last while being under pressure. We want to keep showing up as our best selves. In this section, we'll explore three important lessons, ones that it took me my entire career and current challenges to truly understand. My hope is to help shorten your growth curve so you can sustain better than I did in my most recent years. Through connecting with people farther along this journey, I've learned that resilience under pressure comes down to three things: awareness, balance, and connection. Awareness is noticing what's happening in you before it controls you, balance is choosing a sustainable rhythm that protects against burnout, and connection is building trust and relationships that support you when life's storms hit. Resilience is built one choice at a time.

7

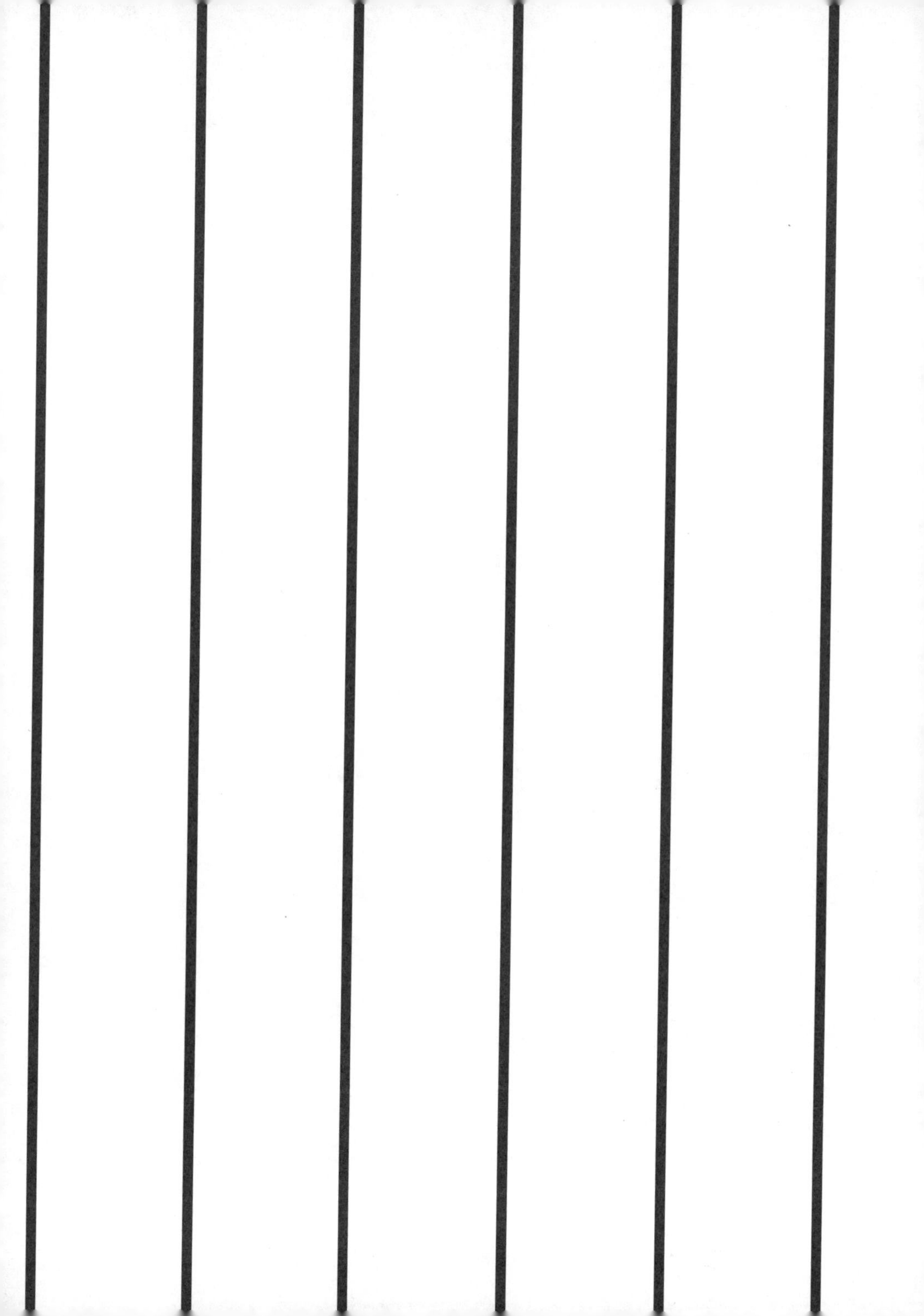

# THE AWARENESS OF A CHAMPION

JUST A WEEK OR SO AFTER THE 2016 WORLD SERIES, I HAD A PANIC attack on my way to Chicago, where I would serve as the parade marshal for the Festival of Lights. That moment began an offseason of mental health struggles with depression and anxiety that I was completely unprepared for and deeply surprised by. After all the success, I began to feel like I was losing part of myself. What do you do after accomplishing everything you ever wanted in your sport? Where do you find the next motivation? As an athlete, I was having an identity crisis on top of trying to deal with all the new expectations of fame. A few days of wallowing in bed to get rest led to weeks of sleepless nights, which led to some scary thoughts. *What is happening?* I didn't feel like myself anymore, and everything that I used to enjoy was feeling like drudgery. I finally started talking to a counselor about everything. Turns out my body wasn't experiencing this newfound achievement as the joy that it seemed on the outside.

I started to learn that one can be so locked in, so present in the moment, so versatile and ready to perform when the bright lights hit. But what other successful leaders don't usually talk about is what can happen right after all of that is over.

My identity was never in baseball itself, but when you do something so hard, for so long, with all your heart—searching for the best version of yourself so you can come through in the clutch for your team, your city, your community—you don't realize how much of yourself you might be exhausting. There's no time in the moment to think about that. You just have to get the job done.

Looking back now, I realize I was draining myself by never stepping away, never backing off to breathe like a human being. I was so focused on being a hero in the moment. And when we think we'll finally get to rest after winning, we quickly discover that's not how it works.

Winning comes with an extra list of expectations, a whole other level of demands.

When I got that big hit in Game 7, I was in a high emotional state. It was like climbing Everest and reaching the summit—eyes fixed on the top, not thinking yet about coming back down. We take in the view, feel the accomplishment, and then realize, *Okay, now how do I get down?* I had spent so much energy getting there, I had no oxygen left to sustain me at the top. And the longer we have to stay there for others, the harder it is to breathe.

I had learned to be whatever the team needed. Now, as World Series MVP, I tried to do the same—flying all over the country, speaking, fulfilling obligations. But I began to realize something I'd never considered: It's not only challenges and losses that can lead to depression. For me, it was *success*—and everything that success and fame suddenly pulled into my world.

From the outside, everyone thought I should be feeling pure joy. But my reality was different. My body and mind were processing the newness, the pace, the attention—and it felt like trauma. The very thing I'd worked my whole life for was now demanding more than I had to give.

That season forced me to learn something I had ignored my entire career: *awareness.* Awareness that my body was signaling distress. Awareness that success can be just as destabilizing as failure. Awareness that I needed a completely different way of sustaining myself if I wanted to last—not just as a player but as a person.

You can build courage and consistency to perform in high-pressure situations, but if you want to sustain yourself through all the successes and failures, you're going to need a greater level of awareness about what's really going on deep inside you. For me, that lesson didn't come from the championship moment—it came in the quiet, in the aftermath, when I finally had to face what I hadn't seen before.

As high performers—especially as athletes—we're used to being aware of our physical bodies. We pay attention to physical cues, and when something feels off, we fix it. The same is true mentally—when our approach feels off, we make adjustments. The older we get, the better we tend to be at recognizing when something needs to change.

But the kind of awareness I'm talking about is *emotional* awareness. It's a deeper level of awareness than most athletes are used to paying attention to. And honestly, we often shut that kind of awareness off because it doesn't seem to serve us in the middle of competition.

True awareness is noticing what's rising in you before it starts to control you. It's natural to be reactive in the moment, but awareness is learning to pay attention to those emotions in the same detailed way you pay attention to the mechanics of your swing.

As athletes, we focus on what gets us feedback—the

physical, the performance. But thoughts and emotions? We often silence, dull, or numb them so we can perform in the moment. Sometimes that's necessary to get the job done, but it's not sustainable over the long haul. Eventually, it catches up with you. That's exactly what happened to me after the 2016 World Series.

If the goal is staying grounded in who you are while the pressure is still happening, then it's not just about bouncing back—it's about staying engaged and not drifting into autopilot.

Habits of reaction are built over years, but awareness brings clarity. It's the ability to pause when you have space to pause and to step forward when it's time to act. Awareness shines a light so you can notice what's happening in your body, your thoughts, and your emotions—and recenter before it's too late.



## How I Learned Emotional Awareness

When I retired and was walking through major personal challenges, I got connected to what I call a "manly version" of empathy training—sharing emotions honestly with a group of men. These men were from all sorts of backgrounds. I didn't know what any of them did for a living. I barely knew anything about them at all other than what they shared in the group. But we were all there to get real and check in with our innermost thoughts and feelings.

It was raw and honest. No fluff. Just telling the truth about where we were. Almost immediately, I saw the benefit. I realized I had had access to everything as an athlete at the highest level—except emotional-intelligence training.

In 2023 I started Champion Forward, a nonprofit that helps teenage athletes, parents, and coaches process the feelings, normalize the failures, and manage the fame that comes with the sports experience.[1] I knew check-ins needed to be part of the work we were doing. In our Ambassador Program, a check-in starts with exploring an emotional chart in front of the group. On this chart are ten basic emotions that everyone can relate to and are commonly experienced, sometimes daily. Each person names the emotions that are current for them in the moment. Sometimes we follow with a sentence of context, but even if we don't, there is still benefit. An emotional release valve is turned on, like letting the human inside breathe a sigh of relief for just a minute. When we are in a team meeting, we start this way. When we are on

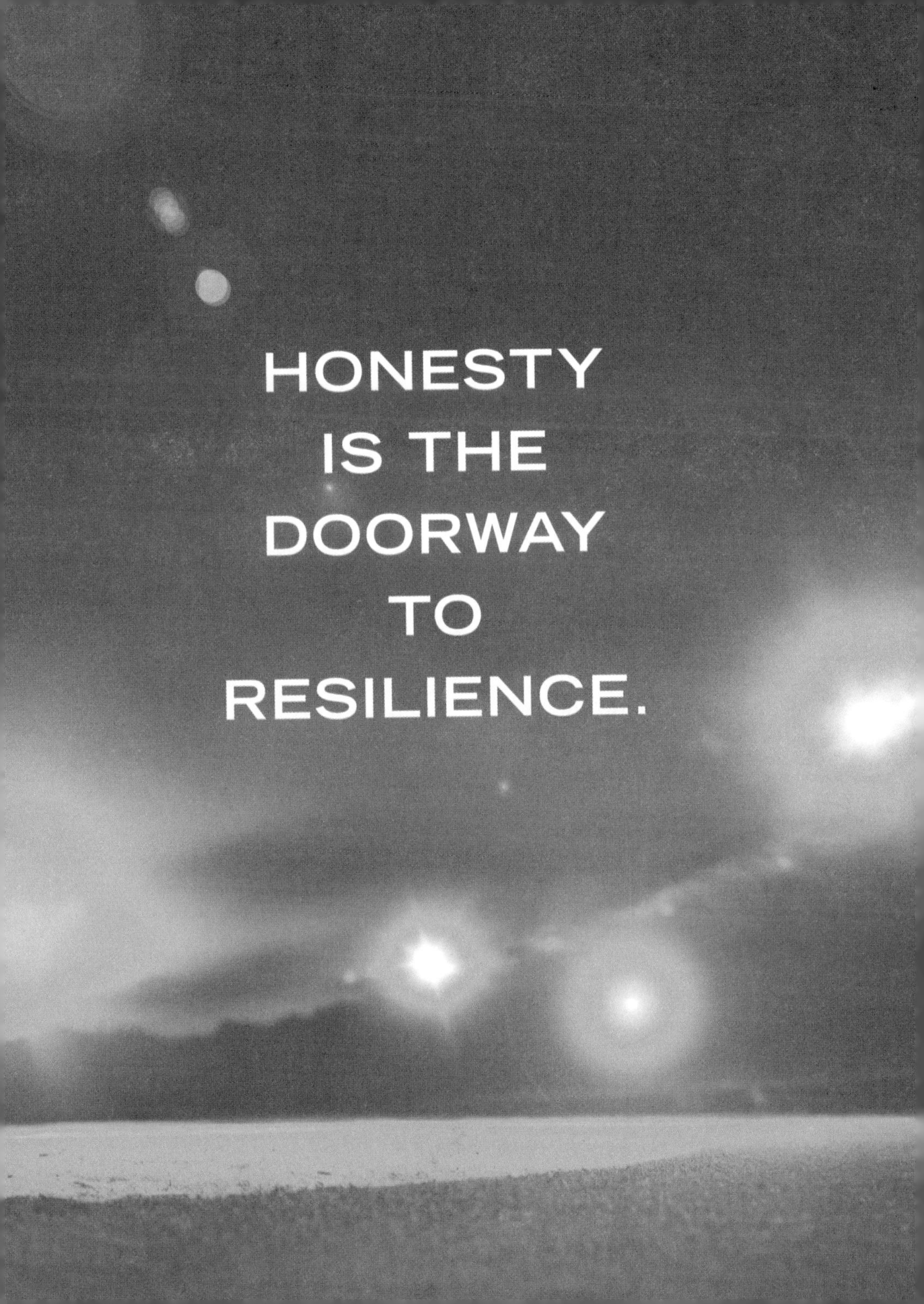

HONESTY
IS THE
DOORWAY
TO
RESILIENCE.

an Ambassador Zoom call, we start this way. And anytime emotions are big enough to threaten the moment with greater pressure? We check in again. It's a constant return and reset for us.

## Why It Works

I believe that true champions have a strong emotional quotient. Recognizing and naming emotions is a competitive advantage. Athletes are trained to fix anything that might challenge their performance. But one of the strongest skills you can learn is to sit with an emotion without trying to change it immediately.

In our Ambassador Program, everyone participates. No matter who the leader is, they check in too. This models honesty and makes it safe for everyone else.

It's not about the backstory. Participants don't have to explain *why* they feel a certain way. One simple word is enough to open the release valve and acknowledge their truth in the moment. Over time, this changes culture. Athletes begin to see patterns. Parents start to understand what's unspoken. Coaches get a real read on their team before making decisions.

Leaders set the tone for whether emotional honesty is valued. Young people are watching to see if we treat transparency as weakness or as something that strengthens the whole group.

This check-in is one of the simplest ways to model that value, praising participants' honesty more than their results. The truth is, everyone struggles.

I've heard it said that there are healthy people and unhealthy people, and the only difference is that the healthy ones can name their dysfunctions. The same is true for groups. It's not about *changing* how you feel in the moment but *naming* it. That skill builds resilience that sustains high performance over the long haul.

There are healthy people and unhealthy people, and the only difference is that the healthy ones can name their dysfunctions.

## The Tension

The emotional tension of awareness is that slowing down feels scary. High performers push forward, stay busy, and grind harder. Stillness feels like weakness, and naming emotions feels like giving them power. So we avoid it—numbing, distracting, or just keeping busy, hoping feelings fade.

But what we don't acknowledge will eventually own us. Ignored emotions don't disappear; they leak sideways as anxiety, anger, exhaustion, or disconnection. Remember, success can be just as destabilizing as failure. After big wins, instead of joy, we might feel panic or depletion. That's the hidden cost of ignoring awareness.

For the rising, the tension often shows up as anxiety before a test or game, fear of letting people down, or exhaustion from carrying expectations. For the rooted, it can be the quiet panic of being stretched too thin—leading at work, parenting at home, or mentoring others while ignoring your own heart.

Being still enough to notice our emotions feels vulnerable. It's uncomfortable. We might even feel ashamed: *Shouldn't I be stronger than this? Shouldn't I be grateful?* But what's needed isn't more toughness—it's courage to stop, notice, and be honest. Awareness requires gentleness, the willingness to sit with what's real instead of suppressing it. That honesty is the doorway to resilience.

## The Activation

Awareness is a skill you can develop. The mental discipline of awareness is learning to notice and name what's going on inside you before reacting.

- **For the rising:** Think about mechanics in sports or school. When your swing feels off, you adjust. When your body signals fatigue, you rest. But with emotions, we often ignore the signals. Awareness flips on the light: *Before I explode, shut down, or run, let me name what I feel.* I wish I had learned when I was younger the importance of paying attention to those emotions instead of avoiding them and seeing them as weakness. I probably would have learned more about myself and been able to contribute in greater ways as a leader on and off the field. It might feel like discomfort now, but it will turn into leadership later.

- **For the rooted:** As leaders and mentors, the same applies. You notice others' performance breakdowns quickly—but often ignore your own inner signals. Awareness means checking in with your emotions before they spill out onto those you lead. If we expect our young people to manage their emotions, we have to set the example. As a parent or coach, we struggle daily when we care so much but have as much growing to do as they do.

One practical tool is the chEQ-in—simply naming emotions in real time: *I feel anxious. I feel hopeful. I feel tired.* This act shifts you from being run by your emotions to being rooted in awareness. Patterns emerge—you see when stress spikes, when joy deepens, and when loneliness lingers.

## The Engagement

Here are three ways both the rising and the rooted can grow in awareness this week:

### Personal (Pause and Name)

- **For the rising:** Set a reminder twice a day—maybe mid-morning and evening—and pause to name three emotions you feel. No backstory, no justifying—just naming. This builds awareness like muscle memory.
- **For the rooted:** Use reminders to notice your feelings, but also model it in front of those you lead. Normalize the practice of naming so others see that strength includes self-awareness.

### Relational (Model Awareness)

- **For the rising:** In a conversation with a teammate, friend, or parent, share one emotion you're carrying (for example, "I feel nervous about tomorrow"). That kind of honesty builds trust.

- **For the rooted:** In a meeting, practice, or family setting, name one emotion honestly—out loud. Vulnerability from you gives permission for others to be real too— and strengthens the group more than pretending.

Spiritual (Embrace Stillness with God)

- **For the rising:** Once this week, practice five minutes of stillness with God. Notice what comes up in your heart, and name it before Him. End with praying, *God, I give this to You.*
- **For the rooted:** Apply the same practice from "For the rising," but extend it as intercession. Name your own emotions, then pray over those in your care, asking God to strengthen them through awareness too.

Awareness isn't weakness; it's wisdom. It doesn't mean you drown in feelings; it means you notice them before they take over. It doesn't mean you quit when life gets hard; it means you're steady enough to keep going with clarity.

Awareness creates choice: Instead of reacting blindly, you respond wisely. This pause builds resilience—not by removing struggle but by helping you endure it with clarity. Psalm 46:10 encourages this commitment to choosing to practice stillness: "Be still, and know that I am God." Stillness isn't laziness; it's space to notice your body, thoughts, and emotions—and then hand them over. God doesn't ask you to fix your feelings; He asks you to bring them to Him. Awareness becomes an act of surrender, strengthening you from the inside out.

The paradox is this: Slowing down makes you stronger. By pausing, noticing, and naming, you gain resilience that outlasts both the highs of success and the lows of failure. And that's the heart of resilient strength: not pretending you're unshakable but being honest enough to notice when you're shaking—and choosing to keep walking forward anyway.

After the World Series, I didn't want to slow down. Honestly, I didn't want to face the emotions that would come up if I did. But that's exactly where God met me. In the stillness. And in that space, I realized He wasn't asking me to fix what I felt. He was asking me to name it, to hand it over, and to trust Him with it. That's when the rebuilding started.

## Moving from Training to Trusting

Awareness isn't just a mental skill; it's a spiritual posture. Slowing down to notice your body, your emotions, and your thoughts is more than self-help—it's surrender. When you bring those raw, honest pieces of yourself before God, He doesn't shame you. He steadies you.

David prayed, "Search me, God, and know my heart; test me and know my anxious thoughts. See if there is any offensive way in me, and lead me in the way everlasting" (Psalm 139:23–24).

That's the heart of awareness. You're not just naming emotions so you can manage them better; you're inviting God to shine His light on them so you can walk lighter. True resilience isn't built by ignoring what's inside you. It's built by slowing down, telling the truth about what's real, and then handing it over.

So here's the challenge: Don't numb, distract, or keep grinding when pressure builds. Pause long enough to be aware, honest, and surrendered. Let God search you, and then let Him lead you.

# INTENTIONAL WALK

1. What emotions have you been trying to push down instead of naming honestly?

2. Where might God be inviting you to slow down so you can hear His direction?

3. How could you model emotional awareness—to your kids, your team, or those you lead—as an act of strength, not weakness?

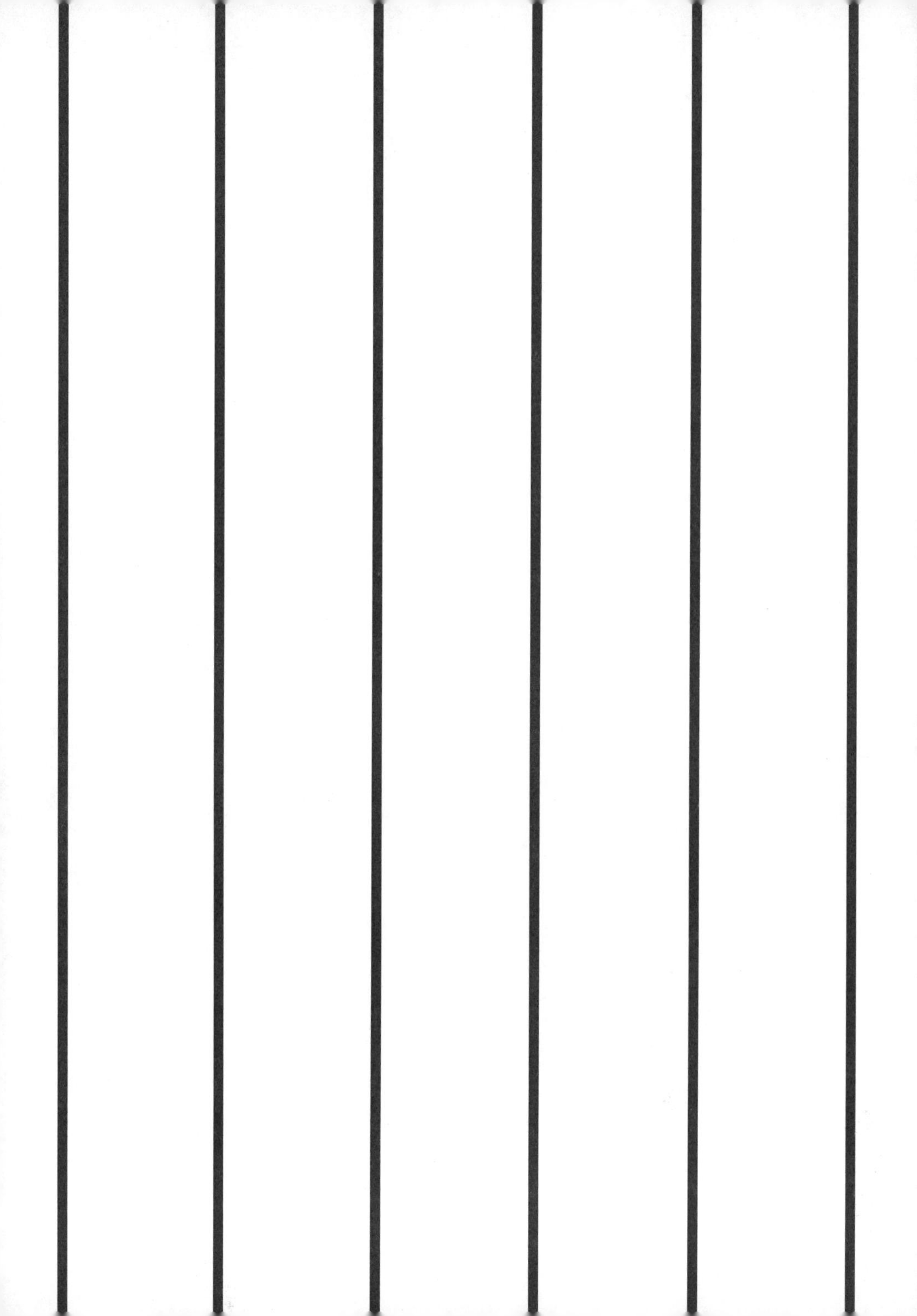

# BREAKING FOR BALANCE

IN MY EARLY TWENTIES, I DIDN'T HAVE A WELL-ROUNDED SET OF activities outside of baseball that gave me a true sense of rest. There wasn't anything that could pull me out of my baseball tunnel and remind me who I was outside the game.

When we pursue a passion that turns into a job, it can consume all our energy. It's not just a hobby—it's our work. That's both a blessing and a curse. We love it so much that we think about it constantly. We work a little too much because it doesn't always feel like work.

Every season I played professional baseball, especially during transition moments, I became like a machine—locked in, laser-focused, prepared every single day to meet the challenge under the bright lights. That helped me perform at a high level. But when the performances stopped, it would take me about two weeks of doing almost nothing to come down from that constant adrenaline high and return to being human again. You can't live in the hero state forever.

Those two weeks were always raw. Multiple years in a row, I found myself in tears during that first stretch of the offseason, never telling anyone. I think it was a kind of shedding—the release of all the effort, the passion, the sweat, the preparation. Knowing the season was over. Accepting that the numbers were what they were. Some years I hit my goals, others I didn't. Either way, there was a breaking inside me. A return to normalcy. A moment of grieving.

Those transitions weren't fun, but I've come to believe they were necessary. They grounded me. They reminded me that life is not about performing. Life is not about producing. When you're so locked in to your passion or your work, you can lose sight of that. Regardless of how much pressure you face each day, you need to create space to transition back to being human. You need to take a break and realize that even if you could produce more for the team, you can handle only so much before you need to let go.

Throughout my career, I had many moments of breaking. But even then, I wasn't fully processing what it looked like to take a complete break *on purpose*. If I'm being honest, I didn't know how to let go of all the expectations other people had for me.

That truth hit even harder after my two World Series Championship seasons. In 2015, with Kansas City, we had our third child two days after I got home. That was my offseason—no decompression, no pause. In 2016, with Chicago, two days after being named the World Series MVP, my agent had five thousand appearance requests for me—opportunities to represent my team, the Cubs organization, and the city of Chicago. Those months became a whirlwind of media, events, and commitments.

Looking back, I can see it clearly: I desperately needed to be alone in the woods for at least a week or two. I needed to come down from the adrenaline, the pace, the constant weight of meeting the pressure day after day. I needed to find my balance again—to rest and restore the energy system I had completely depleted.

I wish I knew then what I know now. If you want to be prepared for pressure, prepare to take a break from it. Balance is not just recovery for your body—it's renewal for your identity. For high achievers, it's not optional. If you want to sustain success over the long

If you want to be prepared for pressure, prepare to take a break from it.

haul and remain resilient, you must learn how to break for balance.

Balance isn't about symmetry or finding the perfect ratio of work to rest. It's about using your awareness to pay attention to your capacity, to what drains you, and to what gives you life.

For years, I thought balance meant having faith, friends, and a few things outside baseball that gave me a break. But I wasn't paying attention to my energy system. When you're performing at a high level and your engine is running in the highest gear, you have to pay even more attention to the maintenance and "garage time" it takes to keep it running.

You might be able to sustain short-term success without balance, but burnout is coming. Injury is coming. Declining performance is coming. And if you're feeling confused or stuck today, there's a good chance you haven't been tracking your energy and taking the rest you need to keep operating at your best.

My own lack of balance contributed to a mental breakdown. I've watched other top performers cope in unhealthy ways—whether that was through substance use, or spending too much money, or unhealthy relationships, or other addictions—because nothing in our system taught us how to balance. Even faith can become another arena to perform—for God, for others, for yourself. In 2016 I began to believe that platform and significance are given to those whom God expects to make something for Him through their extra effort. In other words, when God blesses you, He expects you to do more than just be grateful for it. There's a fine line between doing something for God because He needs you to versus doing it just because you want to. I felt like my platform necessitated doing more for God even though I was tapped out. But that wasn't God. That was me. That's one of the great fallacies of high achievement: believing that more is always better.

If you buy into that belief, you'll chase unnecessary reps. You'll trade enthusiasm for exhaustion. You'll scramble to keep up at every showcase, every tryout, every practice. But true balance doesn't take you *out* of the fight; it prepares you to win it. It builds the sustainability and resilience to make your pace both practical and purposeful when the pressure is highest.

It's like a pitcher who comes out firing all his best pitches in the first few innings. Eventually, he'll slow down, and hitters will figure him out. But the pitcher who knows when to throttle back and when to push forward? That's the guy who's still effective in the ninth inning with the game on the line. Balance is the same way—it's what carries you through the most pressure-packed moments.

It's the job of leaders to track the energy of their group and of individual players. That means checking in regularly so key players don't fade late in the season—or late in the semester, late in the fiscal year, late in a big project.

Just like with awareness, taking a break isn't weakness—it's wisdom. Trust in yourself, in God, and in the process, believing that rest keeps you strong. And use wisdom, knowing when to push and when to pull back. Rising people often need rooted mentors to help them make that call.

But here's the other side of balance: It can't become an excuse. Fear, fatigue, and pressure are not always signs to stop—sometimes they're signs that you're stretching your capacity and growing. If you naturally feel like you aren't giving 100 percent, there's a good chance you may be using your stretch and the discomfort of it to get out of pushing yourself toward growth. If you work yourself to the bone and have trouble giving yourself grace, you are probably the person who is getting close to burnout. Wisdom is what helps you tell the difference between the push that leads to burnout and the push that propels you beyond the discomfort toward growth.

This matters beyond sports. As we get older, we all have to assess our capacity for the pressure in front of us. That requires trust—and wisdom—to take breaks, to keep reserves for the relationships and conversations that matter more than any big-stage performance.

Nobody stays mentally sharp without support. Sometimes we need borrowed belief. Sometimes we need someone to offer us perspective we can't see ourselves. That's why safe spaces to process feelings matter so much. That's why we need mentors, teammates, and guides who can help us through these challenges. And it's why Champion Forward exists—to help people pause, reflect, and find balance in the middle of whatever pressures they're facing.

## The Tension

For many, stopping feels like failure. For high achievers, slowing down can stir up feelings of guilt, shame, and fear. The message of the culture—and often the one in our own heads—is: *Grind harder. Hustle more. Rest later.* So when you pause, it feels like you're falling behind.

For the rising, that might be the guilt of skipping a workout, taking a break from studying, or not always saying yes to every social demand. For the rooted, it often looks like the

PRESSURE PUSHES YOU TO KEEP PRODUCING, BUT YOUR SOUL PLEADS FOR SPACE SIMPLY TO BE HUMAN.

fear of disappointing family, missing opportunities at work, or letting down those who depend on you.

The emotions run deep:

Guilt: *If I take a break, I'm letting people down.*
Fear: *What if the opportunity passes me by?*
Shame: *Strong people don't stop. Leaders don't rest.*

But the truth is, ignoring balance doesn't make you stronger; it makes you brittle. The breaking moments—the tears after a long season, the exhaustion that lingers even after success—are reminders that you can't live in the hero state forever. Pressure pushes you to keep producing, but your soul pleads for space simply to be human.

What's needed isn't more willpower. It's gentleness. It's the humility to admit limits. It's the honesty to say, *I'm not a machine.* And it's the courage to stop when everything in you screams to keep going.

## The Activation

The mental skill here is energy awareness: recognizing what you're carrying, how it's affecting you, and when it's time to pause or push. Most people don't notice until they crash. Awareness means reading the signals before breakdown.

- **For the rising:** Energy awareness helps you see when guilt, fear, or comparison are pushing you too hard. Sometimes fatigue means you're growing. Other times, it's a warning light that you're burning out. Wisdom is learning the difference. I really struggled with this as a young person, and I know I was teetering on being overwhelmed for a long time before it caught up to me. I believe you can do it differently.
- **For the rooted:** Energy awareness means watching for the subtle costs of overextension—irritability with family, emptiness after work, or neglecting your own renewal. It's not selfish to rest; it's stewardship. Though we're wired to believe rest is selfish, if we balance it, it's the first step in caring well for others.

Rest isn't laziness; it's sustainability. It's not just recovery for the body; it's renewal for the soul. Even faith can get twisted into performance—trying to do more for God instead of simply being with Him. That was the trap after the 2016 season—believing more was always better, when what was needed was to let go.

# The Engagement

Balance grows through intentional practices. Here are ways to find balance this week:

## Personal (Identify and Release)

- **For the rising:** Write down two pressures you're carrying. Ask, *Which one am I holding that I don't have to?* Choose to release one: Say no, delegate, or let go of self-imposed weight. Notice how much lighter you feel.
- **For the rooted:** List two pressures you're carrying. Identify one burden you've taken on out of pride, guilt, or fear, and release it. Model for others that strength is found in knowing what to carry and what to lay down.

## Relational (Protect Balance Together)

- **For the rising:** Ask a teammate, friend, or mentor to check in with you about balance. Invite them to remind you when you're pushing too hard.
- **For the rooted:** Invite someone to hold you accountable for rest, and offer the same to someone who's in your care. Create a culture where rest is honored, not shamed.

Spiritual (Practice Sabbath Moments)

- **For the rising:** Block off one hour this week as a Sabbath moment. No phone, no schoolwork, no performance. Just breathe, pray, or walk with God.
- **For the rooted:** Carve out one holy hour, but also pray Matthew 11:28 over those you influence: "Come to me, all you who are weary . . . and I will give you rest."

Breaking for balance isn't weakness; it's wisdom. It doesn't mean quitting your calling—it means creating space to sustain it. Remember, the breaks that feel like you're falling behind are actually what prepare you to endure.

## Moving from Training to Trusting

Balance makes us not only more resilient but more human. And when we stop, release, and renew, we discover the truth: We were never meant to carry it all. We discover what holy balance looks like in the person of Jesus. Trusting Him doesn't eliminate our responsibility—it releases what God never asked you to carry. Resilience comes not from shouldering more but from surrendering more.

Jesus' invitation to His earliest followers is also His

invitation to us: "Come to me, all you who are weary and burdened, and I will give you rest. Take my yoke upon you and learn from me, for I am gentle and humble in heart, and you will find rest for your souls. For my yoke is easy and my burden is light" (Matthew 11:28–30).

Balance isn't just about finding a better schedule or removing a few things from your to-do list. That might give you a short break, but it won't give you the deep rest you really need. You can get that from only one Source, and it's not your coach, your boss, your family, or even your own self-discipline. It's Jesus. He's the only unending Source for the kind of rest that will carry you through every season of life and every situation of pressure. Seasons change. Teams change. Jobs change. Circumstances change. But His rest doesn't change, and it doesn't run out.

When Jesus says, "Come to Me," He's not offering a lighter schedule. He's offering a lighter burden. Those aren't the same thing. A lighter schedule frees up your hours. A lighter burden frees your soul. That's why trusting Him with your pace isn't losing ground—it's finding strength you can't get anywhere else.

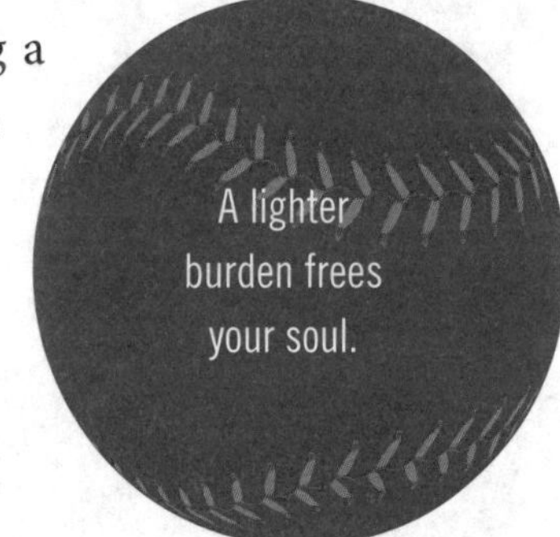

# INTENTIONAL WALK

1. Where am I running on empty right now?

2. What would it look like to trust Jesus with my pace?

3. Who can support me as I aim to guard my balance, and keep pointing me back to Him?

## CHAPTER NINE

# CLUTCH CONNECTIONS

WHEN I THINK ABOUT THAT FINAL GAME OF THE 2016 WORLD SERIES, it's so clear to me that I didn't do it alone. I look at the team that stepped onto the field, the team that was in the clubhouse, and the team that was part of every single process that season. It was a village that hoisted that trophy. And not just the guys on the field either. It was the support staff, the front office, the business office, every scout, every stadium worker, every coach in the minor leagues, every other player. It was a system built on connection and chemistry, and was ultimately a culture that wanted to win together.

As we explore unbreakable bonds in connection, I suspect you're already convinced that your support system—your peers, your teammates, your coaches, your mentors, your parents, the people you advocate for—are all a huge part of your own ability to step into the pressure. The ultimate key to being resilient and continuing to perform when the pressure is greatest is the bonds you build along the way.

Before that final World Series game, just like we had done almost every batting practice since early in the season, our team gathered to the side of the infield. Each time, we'd put our arms around each other—Tim Buss, our strength and conditioning coach, leading the way—and we'd pick one guy to put in the middle of the circle. Then, one by one, we'd go around the circle saying something that we respected, admired, or enjoyed about that guy. Sometimes we'd mention something about his game, but more often it was about who he was as a person—a story, a moment, something we'd noticed. I can remember a few times when I had to fight back my own tears watching the guy be lifted up in words of affirmation by his teammates. I got the feeling in those moments that we should be doing a lot more of that type of thing among men.

It was personal. It was meaningful for every one of us. There was a lot of love shared in those tiny gatherings right before batting practice, and those moments built bonds that stuck with us.

So it was no surprise, in Game 7, when Jason Heyward, one of our team leaders, brought the group together in the weight room at the perfect time—during the rain delay. With the momentum opposite us, we were all feeling the collective weight of failing to hold that lead. We needed someone to speak life and our true identity back into us. We all knew something needed to change, but someone had to say the right thing to get us headed back toward our destiny.

I'll never forget when he said, "It's zero to zero, and none of what happened earlier in the game matters now. Everyone out there knows that we are the best team, but none of that matters right now. What matters is what we believe in this room. All year long we've had each other's backs on that field out there, and we're gonna do it again here tonight, boys." After Jason spoke, what happened was more of the same, like the pregame huddle. Only this time, instead of one guy in the middle, we *all* were in the middle. It was a collective remembering of who we were to each other, what we'd built together, and what we believed we were capable of.

There was, in that moment, a divine connection that took place.

There was, in that moment, a divine connection that took place. That connection, that bond, will live on in my heart and memory for as long as I'm able to remember. And honestly, that camaraderie was the most valuable part of winning the World Series, both with the Royals and with the Cubs. It was the bonds that were built, the coming together to accomplish something special that doesn't come around often.

True connection opens the possibility of creating something special that none of us could create on our own. The collective voice, the collective heart, the collective effort—that's what enables us not only to be courageous but to find consistency and to build resilience together.

## What Connection Really Is

A lot of people think that if you spend time around people and you're part of their group, you're connected. But connection is far more than that. True connection isn't just knowing who the people around you are; it's knowing what matters to them, knowing what's in their hearts, understanding them, and making the effort to find out what makes them tick. Real connection is having a shared goal and a shared process for reaching that goal. And it's built far more in the small, everyday moments—the nuanced, personal encounters that matter to each individual—than in the big, bright-light stage moments.

Sure, teammates have to work together to accomplish

great things when the pressure is on. But true connection is about the trust that's built before you get to that moment so you can depend on each other when the going gets tough. Leaders who build real connection help everyone in the group feel safe to bring their full selves into the team, where every individual is valued for what they bring and support is consistent no matter how someone is performing.

## Connection as the Core of Resilience

This is why connection is at the core of resilience. Every player is going to have rough moments. The question is, does the group believe in them and lift them up when they're struggling? No one is an island, and no one comes through in the clutch every single time. That's why it's so important that the team rallies around the players who make mistakes—because eventually, we all will. I remember making a key error in the ninth inning one year on a road trip that cost us the game. The shame you feel in that moment is real regardless of being a big leaguer. One of the only things that helps is knowing that your teammates and coaches still believe in you when that happens. When several people came up and said, "Don't worry about it, Zo. We'll get 'em tomorrow," it helped me turn the page and get ready to step in with courage again.

When there's a group trust that's pervasive—not only in the clubhouse but also on the field against an opposing team—you develop the kind of chemistry that wins championships. I made bonehead mistakes and felt like I let the team down plenty of times. But I had great teammates who picked me up. That kind of connection gives you the confidence to take big risks in big moments, knowing that if you don't come through, the next guy will. That's how we pick each other up. That's how we have each other's backs. That's exactly what those 2015 and 2016 teams were able to do.

## Chemistry Outperforms Statistics

Some people believe championships are built by assembling a group of individuals whose stats will stack up to wins. On paper, that might be true. But as a player who's been on statistically great teams that didn't come through in the end—and on teams that outperformed the numbers—I can tell you that chemistry matters. The human factor of jealousy, backbiting, and self-centeredness can drag a talented team down. Conversely, enthusiasm, positivity, and endless effort can lift a team above its projections. I've felt both.

## Vulnerability Builds Strength

True connection demands vulnerability. You can't just maintain your "hero self" all the time. Both coaches and players—leaders and followers—have to let their guard down at times and share what's really going on.

One of my great regrets is that I didn't do this more often in my career. Sometimes I was so socially stretched that, when I wasn't in the clubhouse or on the field, I just wanted to be alone. And alone time is okay. But if we want to strengthen our bonds, we need to step in and share transparently, even when we don't feel like it.

When I check in with Champion Forward even as a leader, I make sure I lead with the vulnerable words like *fear*, *shame*, *anger*, and *hope* if I feel them. Leaders—men in particular— often struggle with saying these things out loud, even when we feel them. We are

TRUE
CONNECTION
DEMANDS
VULNERABILITY.

complicated beings who can feel a lot of things at once, tied to different thoughts and experiences. The beauty of what Champion Forward teaches in our check-ins is that you don't have to share any detail if you don't want to, and there's still a level of transparency there. It's about letting people into the human side of what's bothering you or what's driving you. When a player, coach, parent, or leader admits a mistake, it's a humble act that gives confidence to the entire group— because even our leaders recognize they don't have it all together. That humility enables all of us to pick each other up.

## The Discipline of Connection

Connection also takes discipline. We can't leave it to chance or assume someone else will initiate the conversation that needs to happen. I'd rather see players overcommunicating than avoiding communication. Teams or families who avoid communication end up with more dysfunction and more disconnection. Communication is truly the bridge that keeps the group together and focused.

The teams I played on in 2015 and 2016 communicated a lot—not only on the field, in the dugout, and in the clubhouse, but also on the road. Human connection was built

> Human connection was built alongside the heroic relationships we had on the field.

alongside the heroic relationships we had on the field. That's what enabled a leader like Jason Heyward to bring the group together, to remember who we are together, when he sensed the team was struggling.

## Pursue Each Other Under Pressure

The onus is on all of us to pursue each other, not distance ourselves—especially when the pressure is on. Lean in to one another. There will be times when one person needs to communicate and process more than others, and that requires patience. Building the capacity to communicate consistently doesn't come easy—especially for men and especially for athletes. But it's a clear marker of emotional intelligence, of building quality relationships, and of sustaining mental health in the long run. I leaned into my trainer and friend Josh Costello (Provero Performance) more times than I can count or even like to admit. There were plenty of times while training that he had to listen to more than a few gripes and complaints. But as a part of my team, he also shared some of the success. And to this day he is training MLB players in Nashville, providing professional training but also meeting players where they are on their journey.

## The Tension

I'll be the first to admit that opening up and being vulnerable feels risky. Many of us are comfortable being around people—teammates, coworkers, friends—but not truly letting them in. It feels safer to stay on the surface, to keep ourselves polished and protected. Vulnerability stirs fear: *What if they don't accept me? What if I let them down? What if my weakness is used against me?* A young high school athlete named Will comes to mind. He and his dad joined up with Champion Forward Ambassadors to practice some of these skills during a particularly difficult time going through an injury. At our 2024 Champion Forward banquet, he shared how the work had brought healthy connection to his relationship with his family and teammates during a time that would normally draw him toward isolation. He chose to step in and do the inner work despite the stigma around young men sharing their emotions. And I believe the benefit he will experience in the future, should he continue to practice this, will make him a better leader and man for his family and career.

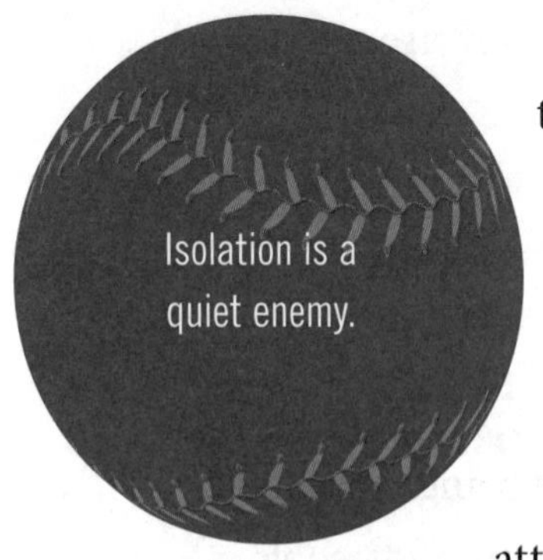


There's also the tension of shame—the lie that says connection makes us needy or weak. High achievers often pride themselves on independence, on shouldering pressure alone. But isolation is a quiet enemy. It convinces us we're safer alone, when in reality it leaves us vulnerable to attack.

For the rising, the tension often shows up as hiding behind performance—being known for your stats, grades, or achievements, but never letting people see your struggles. For the rooted, the tension is the fear of vulnerability as a leader, parent, or coach—believing that if you show weakness, you'll lose respect.

But the truth is, without vulnerability, bonds stay shallow. True connection requires courage—the willingness to be seen for who you really are. And though it feels risky, it's what makes relationships strong enough to withstand pressure.

## The Activation

Relational awareness is a vital part of emotional intelligence. It's the ability to notice, nurture, and sustain bonds that make both you and your group resilient.

- **For the rising:** Relational awareness means going beyond proximity. Just being on a team, in a classroom, or in a friend group doesn't guarantee connection. Awareness means noticing how others are doing, caring enough to ask, and choosing to step in when they need encouragement. In the clubhouse, we used to call it having "court awareness," like you might describe a great passer or defender in basketball. Part of court awareness is being able to notice the energy that people are carrying with them. You don't have to have the answers for them in their challenge, but just showing them that you are aware and that you care makes all the difference in the world. They will remember that down the road.

- **For the rooted:** For leaders, relational awareness means seeing beyond performance. It's asking your players, students, or children not just what they did but how they're really doing. It's slowing down enough to listen deeply, even when your own schedule feels rushed. I get that this is incredibly difficult to do when you feel like you're always running ragged. Slowing down doesn't come naturally to me, and I often struggle doing so, which is why I believe it's so important in building healthy connection. I now understand its connection to our individual and team health.

Relational awareness builds a safety net. When people know they won't be left to struggle alone in the midst of failure, they often find the courage to risk more in pursuit of growth. In order to succeed at the highest levels, you can't play in protect mode. Fear can't be leading the way, and it often does when you feel like no one has your back. But when you build a team full of trust and understanding, watch out! This is why chemistry often outperforms statistics—trust and empathy unlock resilience that talent alone cannot.

Hebrews 10:24–25 reminds us to "consider how" to spur one another on. That phrase signals intentionality—connection doesn't happen by accident. Strong bonds are built on consistent encouragement, honest conversations, and the discipline of showing up even when it's inconvenient.

And here's the paradox: What feels like weakness—vulnerability—actually strengthens the group. When someone admits fear or a leader admits struggle, it doesn't erode trust. It *deepens* it. It signals that authenticity is safe here. That kind of humility creates the strongest resilience of all.

## The Engagement

Connection grows only when it moves into action. Here's how you can live it out this week:

### Personal (Open a Window)

- **For the rising:** Share one honest thing you're carrying with a trusted friend, mentor, or teammate. It doesn't have to be dramatic. Even saying, "I've been anxious about this test" is an act of courage.
- **For the rooted:** Share something vulnerable with someone you trust—maybe another parent, colleague, or fellow leader. Modeling vulnerability teaches others that strength isn't hiding struggle but sharing it.

### Relational (Practice Encouragement)

- **For the rising:** Pick one teammate or classmate and speak encouragement over them—not about performance but about who they are as a person. That kind of affirmation builds trust.

- **For the rooted:** Make encouragement a discipline. Write a note, send a message, or speak face-to-face encouragement over someone in your circle. Your voice carries weight that can steady them under pressure.

Spiritual (Pursue Togetherness)

- **For the rising:** Make time to gather with your community—whether it's in a team, in a small group, or at a family dinner. Read Hebrews 10:24–25 and ask, *How can I show up for others this week?*
- **For the rooted:** Do the same, but extend it outward: Pray specifically for someone in your care, and then let them know you did. Your spiritual presence reinforces their sense of belonging.

Connection doesn't erase pressure, but it changes how you carry it. Alone, pressure crushes. Together, it refines. The Cubs' rain-delay huddle in 2016 wasn't just about baseball—it was about remembering that no one carries the weight alone.

And that's the paradox: The very thing that feels risky—letting others in—is what makes you unbreakable. Independence may look strong, but interdependence is what endures.

## Moving from Training to Trusting

The author of Hebrews reminded us that encouragement, spurring one another on to goodness, doesn't just happen accidentally. Instead, we are to be intentional about it: "Let us consider how we may spur one another on toward love and good deeds, not giving up meeting together, as some are in the habit of doing, but encouraging one another—and all the more as you see the Day approaching" (Hebrews 10:24–25). Plan for encouragement. Purpose helps you to step into it.

"Consider how" is an invitation to slow down long enough to see what the person next to you needs. It's not just showing up when you feel like it. It's showing up because you know your presence might be the thing that keeps someone else going.

In sports and in life, unbreakable bonds aren't built by accident. They grow because people make it a habit to meet, to talk, to check in—not just when it's convenient but especially when it's *not*. That's when it counts the most.

Believers, this is our calling. God hasn't asked us to live our faith quietly in our own lane—He's called us to actively share it and intentionally encourage other believers. That means speaking life into each other, pointing one another back to truth, and refusing to let isolation have the final word.

When pressure hits, you don't rise on your own. You rise because somebody else's voice, presence, or belief steadies your heart. And just like others have done for you, you've got the same assignment—to do it for them.

God uses these bonds to shape us, sharpen us, and carry us through. That's why a quick text, a prayer, a conversation, or sharing a meal is never "just" anything. It strengthens the cord that holds us together.

# INTENTIONAL WALK

1. Who can you "spur on" this week—and how?

2. Are you keeping connection as a habit or letting it slide?

3. Which person in your life needs to hear your encouragement this week?

# YOU CAN BE THAT CLUTCH PLAYER

THE GAME-WINNING DOUBLE BROKE THE TIE, NOT ONLY GIVING THE Cubs that first championship in over a century but earning me the MVP of the Series.

Though I never would have boasted that I was a clutch player, every athlete wants to be known as one. When it mattered most, I simply focused on my process and preparation, which led to an amazing result. I was prepared for the pressure on the field that night. And I believe you can be prepared for your big moment as well.

It may not be in a batter's box. For you, the swing that changes everything might happen in a boardroom. Or it might happen in a delivery room! Your clutch moment could be that important decision you make as you consider your future, weighing the options in front of you. And it might be the way you perform, as a team member, when your *family* is under pressure—whether it's financial, relational, or even as someone you love approaches the end of life. The way you show up in that moment? It will be determined by the way you prepare in *this* moment.

And the way you prepare in this moment may seem a bit counterintuitive. That's because the goal isn't for you to do *everything*. The win in this season is to be intentional about the kind of practice that will equip you to thrive when the pressure comes. Because the reality is that you *can't* do it all. And if you really want to succeed in your passion, you may have to say no to some good things to say yes to something greater and more meaningful. For example, if your social circle is really important to you, you need to choose people who have the same passion to practice that you do. And your preparation might also require sacrifice. I didn't always like missing out on Friday or Saturday night social gatherings, but I consistently chose practice because I knew I was after something more.

Moment by moment, the practice required to win isn't glamorous! It's about showing up for practice. Putting in the work. Remember: Passion without practice is just hype. Practicing with passion? That takes preparation. And preparation will always outweigh the pressure of the spotlight.

What that means for you is that when the spotlight is on—in that clutch moment—you can focus on your process and preparation and see an amazing result. The investment you make today means that you can be prepared for your big moment.

I do want to remind you, though, that there is more to preparing for that moment than constant practice. In fact, for peak performance you need to learn how to stop. Yes— sometimes you need to put everything down and stare at a wall. Or watch the sunset. Or jump in a lake. I want you to seize those opportunities to recharge. But beyond rest and recharging, it's also about finding activities and people who remind you who you are when you're not wearing the uniform—whether you're an athlete, a nurse, a bus driver, or a soldier. These are the family members and friends who keep you grounded.

If you're a leader who's pushing a young athlete, whose body and mind are still developing, you have to help them learn how to make smart decisions. The earlier they learn, the better. That's a big part of what Champion Forward does. We equip parents, coaches, and athletes to have conversations that protect against burnout. We want players to stay optimized and healthy so their journey is rewarding, not exhausting.

When kids are pushed faster and further than is healthy, they burn out. College athletic directors see it every season: Kids who've been recruited to play a sport they once loved may have their first taste of freedom, away from the adults who pushed them too hard, and some of those students choose to quit the sport altogether. I'm grateful my parents never pushed me to the edge just to get to the next level. I'm living proof you can still get your shot—even without being heavily recruited—if you love it, work hard, and find joy in the process. The right doors open at the right time.

The NCAA recently reported that athletes are reporting significantly higher mental health challenges than ever before[1]—and it used to be the opposite. Involvement in sports used to be a mental health advantage. Now NIL (name, image, and likeness) pressure, constant decisions, and impatience with development have flipped that. These younger athletes are dealing with a lot more information, stimulation, and decision fatigue than previous generations. It would make sense if you feel frustrated over this. I know I do. But it's easy to use frustration with the system as a reason to take a break or drop out rather than engaging with your feelings and using these challenges as an opportunity to do the hard inner work to stretch your capacity and grow. As you think about those in your circle whom you influence, I hope you'll share with them some of what you've discovered in these pages.

When I relive that swing that led to the game-winning double, I now can see that it was a natural outcome of the preparation that had come before it. And I want you to feel that same confidence so that when you step up to the plate—when you're under pressure—your preparation will pay off when it matters most.

You got this, and I'm rooting for you. You are capable of becoming the champion you were created to be.

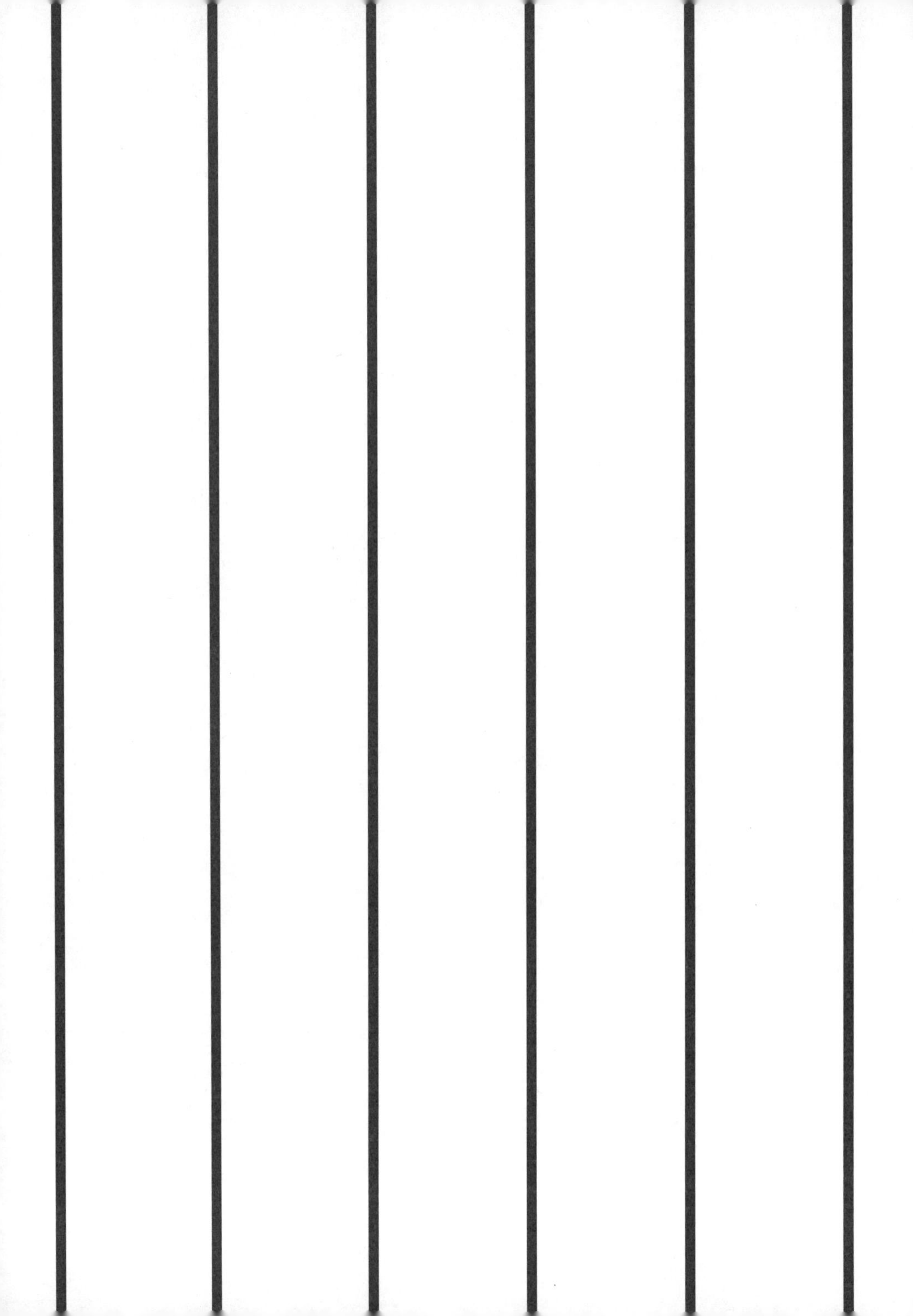

# ACKNOWLEDGMENTS

I WANT TO SAY THANK YOU TO GOD, MY HEAVENLY FATHER, WHO LOVED me when I was in my toughest moments and gave me faith when I didn't have it for myself.

Thank you to Coach Gerdes, Coach Gold, Coach Johnson, Rusty Pendergrass with Houston, Andrew Friedman with Tampa Bay, Billy Beane with the A's, Dayton Moore and the Royals, Bob Melvin, Ned Yost, and last but not least, the Chicago Cubs and Joe Maddon. These people believed in me throughout my career and gave me opportunities to show up to the pressure.

A huge thank you to all the great athletes and teammates I have played with over the years (not the least of which are my 2015 and 2016 championship teammates). You made me better, and I hope I did the same for you.

Thank you to the Fedd Agency for believing in this project and to Thomas Nelson for giving me the opportunity to make this book a possibility.

Thank you to Connor, Brad, Jeff, Rob, and all the men who have walked with me in group emotional awareness work. You have transformed the way I experience loss and have walked with me on this pathway in the challenging heart work of resilience.

I'd like to say a special thank you to John Harrison, who has been a best friend these past few years and has helped me step into my calling in this new season, along with the rest of my team: Liz King, Shauna Kelly, Jordan LaRocca, Adam Jensen, Brett Whitley, Jennifer Masuda, and a host of others in both Illinois and Tennessee who challenge me daily to be the best version of myself in all my new roles while also giving me the grace and space to fail forward.

Thank you to my mom, dad, siblings, and extended family, who have supported me through thick and thin.

And finally thank you to my kids, Zion, Kruse, and Blaise. You continue to be the inspiration for my ongoing growth and desire for healthy connection in this world. I love you.

# APPENDIX

*Additional Notes from the Field*

## CHAPTER ONE

## PASSION TO PRACTICE

## *When Pressure Comes for Us*

ONE OF THE FIRST THINGS ANY ATHLETE LEARNS IS HOW TO TAKE AN athletic stance before the movement ever begins. Your stance must be strong enough to hold its ground when pressure arrives. It's not just a physical position. From a mental standpoint, it's a declaration of being ready—of competitive readiness.

Long before the moment will challenge you, the stance reveals whether you've already *decided* to stand. For me, pressure begins when I wake up for the day. It begins in my preparation. It begins with morning thoughts and self-talk. Doubts are normal. Fear questions what you're really capable of, or sometimes whether you even want to show up.

Before the moment of testing, pressure forces a decision of what you're willing to sacrifice in order to be ready. We know pressure will come for us. We don't get to avoid its assault on our day. So we are either grounded in preparation and ready to step in or we're left hoping we don't get crushed.

Every person doesn't look the same in their stance, but the strongest have tested their stance over time. They can go back to hours of preparation and the repeated decision to step in and stand firm in the box.

A solid stance shows whether someone has chosen to prepare for speed, or whether they're about to get rushed by what's coming at them. That's true physically, emotionally, and relationally.

Standing firm will always cost something. Preparation costs comfort. Readiness costs convenience.

Standing requires choosing what you love enough to carry pressure for. This is the kind of love the Bible calls *agape*: not simply emotion, but sacrificial commitment—the willingness to take up a challenge before the champion is crowned.

Passion shows up best as self-directed readiness. Not excitement. Not motivation spikes. Readiness.

You won't always feel passionate. You won't always feel like you want it. But love, expressed through preparation, allows you to stand even when the feeling isn't there.

Self-directed readiness matters here most. Being ready doesn't mean you're always at peak performance. It means you've chosen to prepare without needing to be pushed. It's the decision to take responsibility for your readiness before someone else demands it from you. You won't simply drift into this kind of readiness.

Self-directed readiness is choosing to stand firm without external pressure. It's preparing when no one is watching. It's practicing when there's no applause. It's staying grounded when the pressure gets loud. Pressure becomes familiar territory.

This stance moment doesn't just show up in athletics. It shows up before hard conversations and leadership moments, and before stepping into relationships that feel uncomfortable.

Maturity isn't about failing less. It's about staying longer in an uncomfortable truth—standing in the gap and choosing responsibility and presence before you know the outcome.

No one can predict how things will turn out, just like you can't know the result of a swing before you take it. But pressure will keep coming. It always does. The real question is whether you've already decided you're willing to stand.

**CHAPTER TWO**

## FAITH THROUGH THE FOG

### *Confidence Without Certainty*

Everyone exercises faith, whether they realize it or not. The difference is that the ones who do it intentionally seem to grow faster—and go farther with it. Most people think that faith just means believing something will work out in their favor. But what they're really wrestling with is wondering, *Can I be committed without knowing the outcome?* We all want to know how something ends before we decide how much of ourselves to give to it.

When clarity is missing, our efforts become cautious. Our engagement becomes partial. And what really seems like wisdom is often just protection. The problem isn't a lack of faith. The problem is an *unintentional* faith. Because the truth is, every day you employ trust.

Confidence is not certainty. It is the trained ability to stay connected and engaged when certainty isn't available. You either trust your instincts, or you trust in a plan, or perhaps you trust that if you hold back and stay guarded, you will be safe. The question isn't whether or not you're exercising faith. It's whether or not you're doing it *on* purpose *for* your purpose.

When you're performing an athletic move—especially a rotational move—this shows up in how you coil the body in preparation for the rotation. Before anything powerful happens, the body must load up its power. This coil isn't passive. It holds tension without panicking. It stays engaged without rushing to let it all go.

When I played baseball, I never knew what pitch was coming toward me as I stood in the batter's box, but I had to be committed anyway. The hitter who refuses to load until they're certain what pitch it is will never be ready to swing with their full power.

Life works the same way. Faith isn't the absence of doubt. It's the willingness to stay loaded and ready, even when doubt is present. It's choosing to engage over detaching. It's trusting in what you've trained for before you see how it turns out.

The athletes who grow fastest aren't the ones with the most certainty. They're the ones willing to stay committed and engaged longer. They don't rush to the outcome, and they don't bail early just because they aren't sure what's coming.

Faith of this nature doesn't make life easier—but it does make you stronger. And strength, built this way, lasts.

## CHAPTER THREE

## STRETCHING FOR PERSPECTIVE

### *Power Under Control*

Most people don't struggle when they don't care. They struggle when they care and experience pressure, and when they have patterns that don't serve them. They have habituated reactions they turn to.

Stress tends to speed us up. So when something goes wrong, our bodies react before our minds have time to choose. The old habits take over. The same swing, same tone, same mistake, again and again.

I've felt this frustration too—not just about the result of my effort, but feeling stuck in a pattern that I can't seem to break.

The problem isn't effort. It's your reaction. Reactions can feel strong and familiar. They happen fast. But a reaction isn't the same as a response. Reaction repeats the past. Response creates something new.

One mental performance indicator—decision-making under pressure—is the ability to slow down the internal response just enough to choose a different action instead of defaulting to an automatic reaction.

So here's the paradox most people miss. Slowing down while under pressure is actually what gives you more control than speeding up. It sounds backward. Pressure seems sped up already, telling you to toughen up or push harder. But the real adjustment doesn't happen at full speed.

In a batter's swing, this is obvious. A batter can see a pitch clearly yet still respond poorly with their body mechanics. Their eyes might be focused, but their body goes where it's been trained to go. That's where a good coach and good video come in to help make an incredible difference.

You need to have some perspective outside your body, the kind that shows what you may not be able to feel or sense from inside. Quality correction won't happen from trying harder. But correction does begin to happen when you are able to see things differently. This type of response has to be learned and then trained. And it requires a kind of quiet, understated strength.

When this happens, a player can start to apply what most strong athletes don't understand: a sense of gentleness. It's having controlled power. Gentleness is the ability to pause, to receive input, to adjust without spiraling or defending yourself. It's learning to choose curiosity over ego. It's learning to stay open long enough for change to take root.

Most people think that *gentleness* means weakness. But in reality, it's the type of strength and intention that gives them options. When you can learn to respond instead of react, this interrupts the pressure from trapping you in the same pattern. You're less likely to end up repeating the same mistakes simply out of habit. You can begin to make adjustments. You actually begin to grow. You can then move forward.

It's no secret that this philosophy applies far beyond a batting swing. This can be used in conversations, conflict, leadership, relationships, anything. When stress hits, reaction closes doors. But response opens them.

The people who continue growing aren't the ones who never mess up. They're just willing to slow down, listen, and choose differently. Responding with gentleness doesn't mean that you care less. It means you're strong enough to hold your power under control. And that's the kind of strength that lasts.

**CHAPTER FOUR**

## FOCUS OVER FLASH

### *Stay in the Stretch*

The average person doesn't struggle because they're lazy or uncommitted. They struggle because they feel rushed to prove something before they're ready. As I've mentioned before, pressure has this tendency to cause us to speed up. Pressure creates urgency. Urgency whispers, *If you don't act now, you'll miss your chance.* So we tend to rush to decisions. We force outcomes. We move before our strength has really formed. We end up calling it *decisiveness* when it's really just being impatient with our own discomfort in the waiting. In these moments, the frustration isn't just that things aren't working out. It's that we actually moved too quickly.

For athletes, this is obvious. We're supposed to speed up, move faster, decide quicker, push to the tension. Get past the uncomfortable middle as quickly as possible. Because waiting feels wrong. It feels passive. Stillness feels weak as well. Stretching feels like wasted time. *Let's get to the action already!* So we rush into action because we're really just uncomfortable with the time it takes to build capacity.

So here's another paradox for you: Waiting is actually how you access more power. This seems counterintuitive in a world that rewards speed. But trust me when I tell you, strength doesn't come from rushing through tension. It comes from staying patient in that tension long enough to make it work in your benefit.

Back to the power swing—that type of power shows up before your front foot ever fully lands. Your weight stays back; your body remains stretched. Nothing seems dramatic as you're drifting, slightly, patiently, toward the fastball. But in that moment, everything is loading. If a hitter rushes forward too early, their power leaks. Their timing breaks down.

That stretch isn't hesitation; it's preparation. Being patient as the ball comes toward you isn't passive waiting. It is disciplined restraint, the ability to hold back your power until the perfect time.

This is what high-level performers call the ability to be present—staying engaged in the moment without rushing ahead of it or abandoning it emotionally. Presence isn't passive. It's the discipline to remain connected to what's happening right now, even when urgency is loud and discomfort is real.

Once again, this shows up in all areas of life. It shows up in our most difficult conversations, in career moves, in house moves, in relationships, and in spiritual development. Growth and change rarely happen on our timeline. Remaining in your stretch doesn't make you slower. It will make you stronger.

When I've failed here, it's usually because I wanted relief more than readiness. Learning to stay present in the stretch has required me to slow my breathing, resist premature decisions, and trust that clarity often comes after patience—not before it.

**CHAPTER FIVE**

## PRESENCE OVER PERFECTION

## *Where X Marks the Spot*

Do people really fall apart because they lack discipline? Or do they fall apart because when things go wrong, they chase fixes instead of alignment?

When pressure rises, attention scatters. Thoughts speed up. Emotions spike. The instinct is to do more, try harder, change everything at once. What feels like problem-solving is often just panic disguised as effort.

The problem isn't intensity; it is more like disorientation.

In my mind, self-talk is the internal language that recenters you or pulls you further off course. Under pressure, the words you repeat to yourself determine whether you return to alignment or spiral into reaction.

When something breaks down, most people search externally for fixes—new techniques, new answers, anything that promises relief from the discomfort. But external fixes rarely restore clarity.

Here's the paradox: The fastest way forward is often returning to center. In the swing, this happens at the X position, where balance, strength, and presence reconnect.

Returning to center is not mechanical first; it's mental first.

What you tell yourself in this moment determines whether your body can settle back into truth.

Without a stable internal voice, effort multiplies confusion. With grounded self-talk, decisions quiet, movements clean up, and presence returns.

This same pattern shows up in conversations, leadership, faith, and relationships. When you drift internally, performance follows.

**CHAPTER SIX**

## VERSATILITY OVER VOLUME

### *The Self-Control to Let Go*

Most people think bad decisions happen because they didn't think through a situation hard enough. In reality, however, many decisions fail because there was no time to think at all. Under speed and pressure, the body moves before the mind can even finish a sentence. The moment arrives quickly and the window closes just as fast, and whatever's been trained takes over.

When people freeze or force a decision, it's rarely because they don't care. It's usually because they didn't trust what their body was instinctually about to do. At this point, the problem isn't necessarily having enough speed or power; the problem is usually the untrained instinct they have.

In my mind, resilience is the ability to recover while the moment is still moving. Adaptability is the ability to adjust in real time without panic. Under pressure, success isn't about controlling the moment; it's about trusting what has been trained when conditions change faster than conscious thought.

The paradox most people miss in this situation is that letting go of control is actually how you gain control. That seems dangerous, especially to high achievers, but the goal isn't to think less. It's to train *so well* that thinking isn't even required in the moment of challenge.

In the baseball swing, some decisions happen so fast—within a hundredth of a second—that you literally don't have time to consciously choose. Your eyes recognize and your body decides to move before your brain can intervene. That ability doesn't come from trying harder in the box. It comes from training adaptable responses deeply enough that the right move is already there.

Self-control at speed isn't restraint; it's readiness. When adaptability is trained, resilience follows. You stop forcing outcomes and start trusting preparation. That's when decisions become clean instead of rushed.

This philosophy applies far beyond a batting swing. In leadership, parenting, conflict, and high-pressure moments, you rarely rise by thinking faster. You rise by training responses that can adapt when things don't go as planned.

Letting go of control doesn't make you passive. It allows trained instincts to lead. That's where real mastery lives.

**CHAPTER SEVEN**

## THE AWARENESS OF A CHAMPION

### *Accountable to Kindness*

You might think that the hardest part of pressure is the moment itself. But often, the hardest part comes immediately after.

The swing has passed.

The decision was made.

The outcome is clear.

And before the body can even finish the motion, the mind is already judging: good or bad, success or failure, worth it or wasted.

When we experience this immediate awareness, it's easy to react, celebrate too quickly, or criticize too harshly. Whatever momentum we built can disappear if we don't interrupt this moment.

I believe the ability to respond instead of spiral determines whether feedback becomes fuel or friction. Under pressure, the goal is not perfection; it's regulation after outcome.

With kinetic movements, experienced athletes know instantly whether contact was clean or off the mark. A skilled hitter doesn't spiral mid–follow through. They finish the rep. They decelerate with control and let the body complete the motion before moving on.

This is why kindness matters. Kindness allows honest evaluation without self-attack. It separates performance from identity while still allowing learning to occur. Harsh self-judgment floods the system with threat and shuts down learning.

When the nervous system settles, information stays accessible. Kindness regulates. Regulation enables adjustment. And adjustment keeps growth moving forward.

This principle applies far beyond athletics. It applies in leadership, relationships, and moments of failure. Pausing is not weakness. It's how elite performers stay accountable without collapsing.

Finish the rep clean. Let kindness do its work. Then move forward.

## CHAPTER EIGHT

## BREAKING FOR BALANCE

### *Staying Open When It's Over*

Finishing anything well is difficult, especially when things go sideways—but it's difficult even when things go well. Most people think feedback is noise—something you can either just accept or reject. But the real challenge is staying open to feedback long enough for it to help.

After an outcome—good or bad—the body naturally wants to protect itself. Pride tightens the body after success. Defensiveness rises after failure. Either way, openness shrinks. And when openness shrinks, growth stops.

In my mind, responding to feedback well is not agreement; it is receptivity. It is the ability to stay open long enough for information to improve performance instead of threatening identity.

In the kinetic chain, power doesn't end at the moment of contact. After the swing, the body must decelerate smoothly. If the body locks up, balance is lost and injury risk increases. A clean finish requires openness so force can dissipate without damage.

The same is true with feedback. When we tense up, justify, or shut down, learning can't land. When we stay open, even imperfect feedback becomes usable.

This shows up in leadership teams, marriages, parenting, and performance environments. The people who grow the most aren't the ones who avoid feedback; they're the ones who don't tense when it arrives.

Finish the rep. Stay open. Let growth keep working.

**CHAPTER NINE**

## CLUTCH CONNECTIONS

### *Better Together*

Strength compounds when it's shared with others. Pressure has a way of isolating all of us. After a success, pride pulls us inward. And after failure, shame does the same. Either way, our instinct is to carry all the weight alone.

In these moments, the issue isn't independence; it's isolation. When people isolate, their perspective shrinks. Burdens grow heavier. Confidence becomes fragile without reinforcement beyond internal resolve.

I believe being a cohesive team and communicating well is the ability to stay connected under pressure. Communication allows strength, perspective, and accountability to be shared so pressure doesn't rest on one person alone.

In high-performance environments, no one finishes strong in isolation. Teammates help distribute pressure. Coaches stabilize emotion. Shared rhythm keeps effort grounded in reality.

Affirmation from trusted people isn't flattery. It's truth spoken at the right time to steady identity when outcomes try to redefine it.

This principle applies beyond sport. It applies in leadership, seasons of responsibility, and moments where clarity feels thin.

The strongest cultures aren't built on individual brilliance but on people who reinforce what matters *together*.

Pressure doesn't ask you to prove you can stand alone. It invites you to discover how strong you are *together*.

# NOTES

Chapter 3: Stretching for Perspective
1. Athletes in Action, https://athletesinaction.org/.
2. *Vantage Point*, written by Barry L. Levy, directed by Pete Travis (Columbia Pictures, 2008).

Chapter 7: The Awareness of a Champion
1. Champion Forward, https://www.championforward.org/.

Conclusion
1. Greg Johnson, "Mental Health Issues Remain on Minds of Student-Athletes," NCAA, May 24, 2022, https://www.ncaa.org/news/2022/5/24/media-center-mental-health-issues-remain-on-minds-of-student-athletes.aspx.

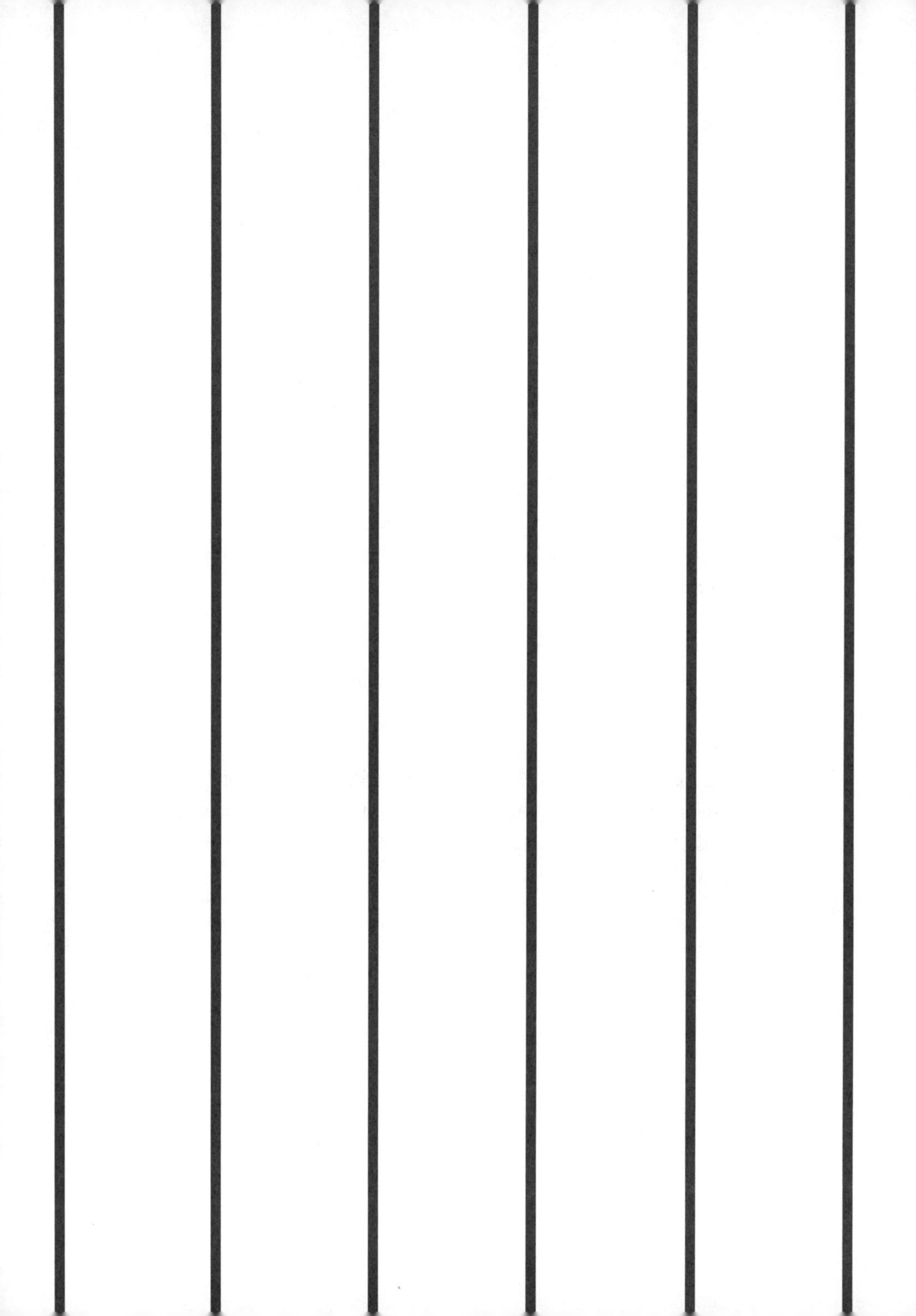

# ABOUT THE AUTHOR

**BEN ZOBRIST** IS A FORMER MAJOR-LEAGUE BASEBALL PLAYER AND two-time World Series champion (including Series MVP). Over his fourteen-year career, Ben played for the Tampa Bay Rays, the Oakland Athletics, the Kansas City Royals, and the Chicago Cubs, earning three All-Star selections. Known for his ability to play multiple positions effectively, he brought a unique blend of skill and adaptability to the game. During his playing career, Ben faced many challenges, including physical injuries and mental health issues. After retiring from baseball, he decided to focus his time, energy, and attention on learning more about the mental and emotional side of being human. This led him to launch Champion Forward, a nonprofit organization that allows him to live out his passion of positively impacting and serving the sports community. As a mental and emotional health advocate, Ben is committed to sharing his story and empowering others to learn, grow, and heal from mental and emotional health issues. His desire is to help teenage athletes, parents, and coaches experience the sports journey in a healthy, sustainable, and successful way. He is a keynote speaker (and now author), Z versatility coach, Chicago Cubs ambassador, hospitality farmer, and self-prescribed D-uber (Dad uber). He loves camping, hiking, rucking, snowboarding, and anything outdoors. He lives in Franklin, Tennessee, with his three children.

For inquiries about speaking,
being coached by Ben,
or connecting with Champion Forward,
visit championforward.org.